VOLUME 2

HOLY LOVE: A WESLEYAN SYSTEMATIC THEOLOGY

Trinitarian Theology

by

Allan Coppedge

John N. Oswalt, senior editor

Christianne Albertson & Matt Ayars, associate editors

VOLUME 2

HOLY LOVE: A WESLEYAN SYSTEMATIC THEOLOGY

Trinitarian
Theology
by
Allan Coppedge

John N. Oswalt, senior editor
Christianne Albertson & Matt Ayars, associate editors

Francis Asbury Press
Wilmore, Kentucky

Published by The Francis Asbury Society
ISBN 978-0-915143-70-2
Printed in the United States of America

To order this book, go to www.francisasburysociety.com or contact:

PO Box 7
Wilmore, KY 40390–0007
859–58–4222
800–530–5673
fas@francisasburysociety.com

Contents

ABBREVIATIONS 7

PART 2: THEOLOGY

INTRODUCTION: New Testament Foundations for the Trinity 10

    Traditional Approaches to Trinitarian Data 11
    Fresh Approaches to Trinitarian Data 12

CHAPTER 1: Old Testament Preparation for the Trinity 26

    The Promises of a New Covenant Prepare the Way for a
        Triune Theism 26
    Plurality Within Unity 27

CHAPTER 2: The Development of the Doctrine of the Trinity 40

    Motivation for Articulating the Doctrine of the Trinity 40
    Historical Issues Behind the Doctrine of the Trinity 41
    The Church's Response to Inadequate Theology 46
    Two Approaches to the Trinity 49

CHAPTER 3: The Triune God in Relation to Creation 54

    Crafting the Terminology 54
    Two Approaches to the Trinity 55
    The Economic Trinity: *Opera ad Extra* 57

CHAPTER 4: The Triune God Within Himself 68

    How the Economic Trinity Reveals the Ontological Trinity 68
    The Ontological Trinity: *Opera ad Intra* 70
    The Mystery of the Trinity 78

CHAPTER 5: The Nature of the Triune God..85

Holiness of the Triune God: The First Indicator of the Being
(*ousia*) of God..86
Love and the Holy, Triune God: The Second Indicator of the
Being (*ousia*) of God 89

CHAPTER 6: The Personal and Moral Attributes of the Triune God........94

The Attributes of the Holy and Loving Triune God........................94
The Personal Attributes of the Triune God....................................96
The Personal and Moral Attributes of the Holy, Triune God 108
Summary of the Moral Attributes 114

CHAPTER 7: The Relative and Absolute Attributes of the Triune God...115

Holiness as Power: the Relative Attributes of God 116
Holiness as Separation: the Absolute Attributes of God...........123
The Nature of the Triune God 132

CHAPTER 8: The Roles of the Triune God...134

How Do We Know the Supranatural God?....................................134
The Roles of the Triune God 137
The Trinity and Foundational Roles..139

CHAPTER 9: The Triune God's Work of Providence................................141

The Function of Providence...141
Three Components of Providence..143
Jesus as the Model: The Way of Understanding Providence...................146

BIBLIOGRAPHY 164

INDEX 172

Abbreviations

ANF   *The Ante-Nicene Fathers.* Edited by Alexander Roberts and James Donaldson. 10 vols. New York: Charles Scribner's Sons, 1925.

BE Works   *The Bicentennial Edition of the Works of John Wesley.* 25 vols (to date). Edited by W. Reginald Ward and Richard P. Heitzenrater. Nashville: Abingdon, 1976–.

EDT   *Evangelical Dictionary of Theology.* Edited by Walter Edwell. Grand Rapids: Baker, 1984.

IDB   *The Interpreter's Dictionary of the Bible.* Edited by George Arthur Buttrick. 4 vols. Nashville: Abingdon, 1962.

ISBE   *The International Standard Bible Encyclopedia.* Edited by Geoffrey W. Bromiley. Revised edition. 4 vols. Grand Rapids: Eerdmans, 1979–95.

NBD   *New Bible Dictionary.* Edited by J. D. Douglas. 2nd ed. Wheaton, IL: Tyndale, 1962.

NDT   *New Dictionary of Theology.* Edited by Sinclair B. Ferguson, J. I. Packer, and David F. Wright. Downers Grove, IL: InterVarsity, 1988.

NIDNTT   *New International Dictionary of New Testament Theology.* Edited by Colin Brown. 4 vols. Grand Rapids: Zondervan, 1975.

NPNF   *A Select Library of the Nicene and Post-Nicene Fathers (NPNF) of the Christian Church.* First Series. 14 vols. Edited by Philip Schaff. Second Series. 14 vols. Edited by Philip Schaff and Henry Wace. 1886–1900. Reprint, Grand Rapids: Eerdmans, 1979.

NSRE *The New Schaff-Herzog Religious Encyclopedia.* Edited by Samuel Macauley Jackson. 13 vols. Grand Rapids: Baker, 1949–50.

TDNT *Theological Dictionary of the New Testament.* Edited by Gerhard Kittel and Gerhard Friedrich. Translated by Geoffrey W. Bromiley. 10 vols. Grand Rapids: Eerdmans, 1964–76

TDOT *Theological Dictionary of the Old Testament.* Edited by G. Johannes Botterweck and Helmer Ringgren. Translated by Geoffrey W. Bromiley et al. 14 vols. Grand Rapids: Eerdmans, 1974–2004.

TWOT *Theological Wordbook of the Old Testament.* Edited by R. Laird Harris, Gleason L. Archer Jr, and Bruce K. Waltke. 2 vols. Chicago: Moody, 1980.

ZPEB *Zondervan Pictorial Encyclopedia of the Bible.* Edited by Merrill Tenney. 5 vols. Grand Rapids: Zondervan, 1975.

PART TWO

THEOLOGY

Allan Coppedge, PhD

To my daughter, Christianne Albertson, with deep appreciation for the privilege of working together as father and daughter on the Trinity and the family language that comes from a heavenly father and gives direction to all Christian theology. It has been a rich blessing as an intergenerational family team to have Cricket's love, encouragement, and critical assistance in crafting the theology of this book. No father could be more proud than I am of her ability to think, shape ideas, and articulate truth in writing while applying the theology of a holy and loving, triune God in her personal life, in her family, and in her ministry to others. In gratitude for being her father and for all she has done to make this work possible, I dedicate it to her with the love of a father's heart.

Introduction: New Testament Foundations for the Trinity

A LONG TRADITION IN the history of the Christian church ties our understanding of who God is to the person of Jesus (John 1:1, 14, 18; 14:9). Jesus, then, becomes the key to organizing the New Testament material about the nature and personhood of God.

The monotheistic faith of Israel provides the background for understanding Jesus. Israel as a people had come to believe in only one God (Deut. 6:4) in distinction from the polytheistic faith of all of the peoples around them. Yet, the Gospels open with references to Jesus as the Son of this God in a unique way (John 1:14–18; Luke 1:35; Matt. 1:18, 20; 2:15). How can Yahweh, the only true God, have a Son? How can a monotheistic God be plural?

Suggestions of this plurality of divinity are found throughout the Old Testament. One component is the promise of a New Covenant to replace the Old, including crucial elements like the coming of a Messiah with the Spirit of God, along with reference to the personal presence of God coming in a new way among his people (Ezek. 37). So, the Old Testament sets the biblical stage for New Testament materials about the Trinity.

The coming of Jesus in the incarnation, coupled with the work of the Spirit at Pentecost, made it possible for the Apostles to lead the New Testament church into an understanding of God in a triune way. This new conceptualization of God becomes a presupposition that underlines their whole way of thinking—sometimes consciously expressed, at other times unconsciously presupposed.[1]

TRADITIONAL APPROACHES TO TRINITARIAN DATA

At times the New Testament portrays all three persons of the Trinity together. The traditional discussion of these Trinitarian passages categorizes them in terms of a "Trinitarian formula" (Matt. 28:19–20, 2 Cor. 13:14, and Rev. 1:4–6) and specifies a "Triadic form" including all three members (Eph. 4:4–6, 1 Cor. 12:3–6, 1 Pet. 1:2). Finally, a number of places make generalized reference to all three persons without a Trinitarian formula or Triadic form. In fact, all three persons are mentioned in this way by every New Testament book except James and 2 and 3 John.

Unfortunately, such an approach to Trinitarian passages (mere classification by formula) results in an entirely inadequate presentation of data. This method suggests that the references to the Trinity are confined to only a few passages of Scripture that may be dispensed with as of only passing interest to the Christian church. This traditional approach carries with it at least two other problems. First, only passages naming all three persons are considered because the literary structure controls the discussion. The more generalized mention of the persons of the Trinity within a passage is not extensively used. Second, and more significantly, the theology of the passages is not given appropriate consideration. Because literary structure controls the discussion, the theological issue of how the persons of the Trinity are related is minimized. The New Testament and the early church handled the data in a much broader

---

1. For a theological evaluation of the biblical materials beginning with Jesus and leading to the triune God, see T. F. Torrance, *The Christian Doctrine of God*, 32–72.

way. If we use their approach as a model, the formula method is far too limited.

FRESH APPROACHES TO TRINITARIAN DATA

In order to adequately handle the significant data of the New Testament on the Trinitarian nature of God, three proposals are in order. First, we must broaden our understanding of the literary structure to include the theology of the persons of the Trinity in the selection of data. Second, we must consider the literary structure of whole New Testament books in light of Trinitarian references. Third, Jesus' challenge to his disciples in the Great Commission will serve as a lens for organizing other Trinitarian passages that refer to all three persons of the Trinity. In combination, these three guidelines will allow us to use literary structure to understand the meaning and theology of the passages.

BROADEN THE LITERARY STRUCTURE

Following the New Testament and early church, we must do justice to all of the scriptural material, so not only must those traditional passages that include all three persons be examined but also passages including Jesus and the Father, Jesus and the Spirit, and the Father and the Spirit.[2]

The whole Trinitarian question arises out of an attempt to understand Jesus' relationship to the Father. Who this Jesus is and how he is related to God is a central issue of gospel proclamation. These questions forced the early church to formulate the doctrine of the Trinity in the fourth century. If Jesus is divine, then the whole understanding of a monotheistic God must be transformed. But we must also consider the relationships of the other two persons of the

---

2. For alternative ways of organizing the references, see Grudem, *Systematic Theology*, 231ff; Oden, *The Living God*, 194ff.

Trinity. This means we must discover how Jesus and the Father each relate to the Spirit.

Using all the passages of Scripture that relate to at least two members of the Trinity broadens the biblical basis for our discussion, but it also gives us a more realistic appraisal of scope of the date that the New Testament church examined. If an implicit Trinitarianism underlies the whole of the New Testament, it should not surprise us that references to all three persons in the same passage are not common.

JESUS AND THE FATHER

Of the four types, the passages identifying the relationship of Jesus to his Father are the most numerous.[3] These may be grouped under six headings. First comes the introduction of Jesus at birth. He is introduced as "Immanuel" ("God with us"; Isa. 7:14; Matt. 1:23), an immediate identification of Jesus with God. The employment of family language develops this identification: "Out of Egypt I called my son" (Hos. 11:1; Matt. 2:15). For the Hebrew audience, such language recalls the relation of God as Father to Israel, now designating Jesus as Son of God.

Second, this relationship of Jesus to Yahweh is described most often by Jesus himself when he uses the phrase "my Father" (Matt. 7:21). When Jesus refers to God's rule as "my Father's kingdom," he redefines the Hebraic conception of the Messiah (Matt. 26:29). The intimacy of this family connection between Son to Father is accented in a special way in the garden of Gethsemane when Jesus refers to his Father as Abba (Mark 14:36). When Jesus speaks to God as Father, he implies a divinity for himself, an implication that is not lost on those around him (John 5:17–18).

The third description of Jesus' relationship to God is as a Son. As Jesus speaks of God as Father, so is he referred to as the Son of

---

3. On whether Father/Son language is time-bound, see Pannenberg, *Systematic Theology*, 1:262–65.

the Father (John 1:49: Matt. 8:29; 14:33).[4] When Jesus questions the disciples about his own identity, Peter confesses him to be both Messiah and "the Son of the living God" (Matt. 16:16).[5] The New Testament reiterates the connection between Jesus as the Son of God and as the promised Messiah (Matt. 26:63; 27:40, 54; John 11:27; 20:31). This connection is sometimes made by Jesus himself with the claim, "I am the Son of God" (Matt. 27:43; John 10:36; 11:4).[6]

The fourth component of Jesus' relationship to the Father comes in descriptions of the way the Son reveals the Father. The key passage in the Synoptics, one that heavily influenced the early church fathers, is Matthew 11:25–27:

> At that time Jesus said, "I praise you, Father, Lord of heaven and earth, because you have hidden these things from the wise and learned, and revealed them to little children. Yes, Father, for this is what you were pleased to do. All things have been committed to me by my Father. No one knows the Son except the Father, and no one knows the Father except the Son and those to whom the Son chooses to reveal him."

John also makes clear that the coming of Jesus provides an adequate image of what God the Father is really like. "No one has ever seen God, but the one and only Son, who is himself God and is in closest relationship with the Father, has made him known" (John 1:18). Jesus declares that he is the only one who has seen God and comes from God (John 6:39, 46; 8:18, 19, 38; 10:15; 13:3), and

---

4. For the theological implications of these passages that relate to the Father and the Son, see Ralph Del Colle, "The Triune God," in *The Cambridge Companion to Christian Doctrine*, 123–25.

5. Cf. the discussion of N. T. Wright and the three possible meanings of the concept "son of God" in the first century: 1) A description of the Messiah as son of God might not necessarily carry divine overtones; 2) in the pagan world where it was the Roman emperor described as son of god; and 3) the glowing implications of the resurrection of Jesus that the title son of God does carry divine overtones. Wright concludes that the resurrection symbolized in particular by Thomas' confession in John 20:28 means that the use of this title is a divine indicator. (*The Resurrection of the Son of God*, 673, 723–36).

6. For the centrality of the role of the Son for understanding the Trinity, see Brunner, *The Christian Doctrine of God*, 209–214.

HOLY LOVE: A WESLEYAN SYSTEMATIC THEOLOGY

he declares to Thomas that to know him is also to know the Father (John 14:7). As he says to Phillip, "Anyone who has seen me has seen the Father" (John 14:9).

Fifth, Jesus does what the Father does. "My Father is always at his work to this very day, and I too am working" (John 5:17). This work includes the divine prerogatives of giving life and exercising judgment (John 5:19–29).

Finally, this relationship between Jesus and the Father comes into focus when he speaks of being one with the Father, "that you may know and understand that the Father is in me, and I in the Father" (John 10:38; see also 14:10–11; 17:21). When Jesus describes his being in God ("I and the Father are one," John 10:30), his hearers understand this as a claim to divinity and accuse him of blasphemy, "because you, a mere man, claim to be God" (John 10:34; cf. 10:35, 38; 17:11, 21, 22). The "I am" sayings of Jesus are given against the backdrop of the great declaration of Yahweh about himself as the "I AM WHO I AM" (Ex. 3:14). When Jesus declares, "Before Abraham was born, I am" (John 8:58), they again attempt to stone him for blasphemy because they clearly understand he is identifying himself with Yahweh of the Old Testament.

This identification of Jesus with God the Father is so strong during his own lifetime that the apostolic witnesses throughout the New Testament affirm it repeatedly (Phil. 2:5–11; Col. 1:15–20; Heb. 1:1–8; 2 Pet. 1:16–17; 1 John 1:2–3; 2:22–24). In the prologue to his Gospel, John sees Jesus (the Word) as one with God before the creation of the world: "In the beginning was the Word, and the Word was with God, and the Word was God" (John 1:1). Paul affirms this oneness of God to the Corinthians: "There is no God but one" (1 Cor. 8:4). "Yet for us there is one God, the Father, from whom are all things and for whom we live; and there is but one Lord, Jesus Christ, through whom all things came and through whom we live" (1 Cor. 8:6). Paul identifies one God, but then in the same breath, he identifies the one Father with the one Lord Jesus Christ. Both of these persons are identified as the divine creator from whom and through whom all things exist. Clearly for Paul this monotheistic God includes both a Father and a Son.[7]

This extensive data on Jesus' relationship with the Father becomes the focal point of discussions with the Arians in the fourth-century debate over the full divine nature of Jesus. While many of these passages do not discuss all three members of the Trinity, the relationship of Jesus to the Father is central in the development of Trinitarian thinking in the early church. The conclusion demanded by these materials is that Jesus, as well as the Father, is divine.[8]

Jesus and the Spirit

The biblical passages that address the relationship between Jesus and the Spirit also come under six headings. The first is the incarnation. This supranatural conception by the Spirit with the Virgin Mary in both Matthew and Luke indicates that the story of Jesus begins with a divine-human interaction (Matt. 1:13, 20; Luke 1:35).

Second, Jesus' baptism introduces his ministry, including the role of the Spirit who visually descends as a dove, symbolizing the anointing and controlling work of God the Spirit on the life of Jesus. Closely connected, John the Baptist witnesses that the one on whom he saw the Spirit descend will be the one who baptizes with the Spirit (John 1:32–33; cf. Matt. 3:11; Mark 1:8; Luke 3:16).

---

7. For the discussion of the role of God as Father in relationship to Jesus, see Wainwright, *The Trinity in the New Testament*, 44–50. The significance of this connection appears when we observe that every epistle in the New Testament but three begin with a reference to God as Father and to his relationship to Jesus. Of the three that do not refer to God as Father in the greeting, two of them refer to him in the early paragraphs of the first chapter (James and 2 Pet.). Only 3 John does not have a reference to God as Father, but it does use family language like "brethren," borrowed from the concept of God as Father. So the norm for the apostolic epistles is that we now understand God as Father and Jesus as his Son.

8. For discussion of how the New Testament focus on God as Father leads to the significance of the role of God as Father for Christian theology, see Kasper, *The God of Jesus Christ*, 50–51.

Third, the early emphasis on the fullness of the Spirit at his baptism (Luke 3:22) directly connects Jesus' ministry with the work of the Spirit. After Jesus' desert experience of resisting temptation by the power of the Spirit (Luke 4:1–14), he begins his teaching in Nazareth with the explanation: "The Spirit of the Lord is upon me, because he has anointed me. . ." (Luke 4:18; Isa. 61:1–2).

Jesus' teaching about the Spirit is the fourth significant category. One comes into a relationship with the Spirit by asking the Father for the Holy Spirit (Luke 11:13).[9] Jesus casts out demons by the Spirit of God (Matt. 12:28; Luke 11:20), and he warns about the blasphemy against the Spirit that will not be forgiven (Matt. 12:22–37; Mark 3:28–30). Further, Jesus alerts the disciples that the Spirit will speak through them (Luke 10:18–20; Luke 12:11–12; Mark 3:11), and this is related to the Spirit's work of revelation (Matt. 22:43). Jesus also views the Spirit as the agent of the new birth (John 3:3–8) and looks forward to the time when the Spirit will flow out of the heart of believers after his own glorification (John 7:37–39).

The fifth area is Jesus' final farewell to his disciples, where he both explains the fuller work of the Spirit and promises to send the Spirit. The Spirit will be a paraclete like Jesus (John 14:16), who will both teach and bring to remembrance Jesus' own words (John 14:26; 16:13–14).

Finally, Jesus is connected with the Spirit in sending forth the disciples. As he sends them out to do the work he was sent to do, he breathes on them, symbolizing the breath or Spirit of God, charging them, "Receive the Holy Spirit" (John 20:21–23).

Among those references that connect Jesus with the Spirit, two seem to bracket the gospel story: the role of the Spirit in the incarnation (Matt. 1:18, 20) and Jesus' sending forth disciples in the same way the Father sent him (John 20:21–22). At the same time, these two events emphasize the sharing of the divine nature

9. Note the context: Luke 10:21–11:13.

between Jesus and the Spirit. Paul strengthens this connection by describing the Holy Spirit as "the Spirit of the Lord" in the same context where he twice identifies the Lord as the Spirit (2 Cor. 3:17–18; see also Acts 2:33, 10:38; Rom. 8:2, 9:1; Gal 3:14, 5:5–6, 5:22–24; Eph. 1:13–14, 3:5–6; 1 Pet. 1:11). These passages from the Gospels, Acts, and Epistles guided the early church leaders as they tried to see the coherence of the biblical data related to all three members of the Trinity. They could not divorce the divinity of the Father from the Spirit, and when Jesus and the Spirit are so closely identified with each other, the divinity of both is reinforced.

THE SPIRIT AND THE FATHER

The Gospels not only speak of Jesus' relationship to the Father and the Spirit but also point to the special relationship between the Spirit and the Father. While this relationship does not receive the same attention as the others already mentioned, it is an important part of the data that relate all three members of the Trinity to one another.

Several times Jesus calls attention to the special relationship between the Spirit and the Father. In one place, the Father longs to send his Spirit to those who ask him (Luke 11:13). Another declares that it will not be the disciples who speak but "the Spirit of your Father speaking through you" (Matt. 10:18–20). The fact that it is "the Spirit of the Father" means the identification is incredibly close. John's reference to "God is Spirit" in John 4:24 may have a double meaning. Certainly, the Godhead is a spiritual being, but John may also imply that God is the Spirit (i.e., God has a Spirit). This can be noted in Jesus' statement to the Samaritan woman, which is one of the strongest statements about the shared divine nature between the Father and the Spirit (see John 4).

Much discussion surrounds the sending of the Spirit. The Father certainly sends the Spirit in answer to Jesus' prayer (John 14:16), and, Jesus in sending forth his disciples links the promise of the Father (Luke 24:47–49) with the baptism of the Holy Spirit (Acts 1:4–5). Surely the promise of the Father under the old covenant relates to the coming role of the Spirit under the new covenant (Isa. 59:21; Ezek. 11:19; 36:26–27; 37:14). Paul associates the work of God with the work of Spirit when he writes, "because God's love has been poured out into our hearts through the Holy Spirit, who has been given to us" (Rom. 5:5). Reiterating this association, he describes the Spirit of God as the one who can reveal God's thoughts (1 Cor. 2:10–15). He further reinforces this relationship between Father and Spirit when he writes of God's temple and God's indwelling Spirit: "Do you not know that you are God's temple and that God's Spirit dwells in you?" (1 Cor. 3:16; 6:19 ESV). Other New Testament passages underscore this strong connection between the Father and the Spirit (Rom. 8:27; 15:13; 1 Cor. 2:4–5; 14:2; 2 Cor. 5:5; Eph. 6:17; 1 Thess. 4:8; 2 Pet. 1:21). The close identification between Father and Spirit is part of the data the early church used in establishing the full Trinitarian understanding of the nature of God.[10]

Implications

All three persons of the Trinity participate in the incarnation, and the resulting life of Jesus is recorded in the Gospels. Sometimes all three are grouped together, but often only two of them are described in their relationship to each other. These Trinitarian passages either refer to Jesus' relationship to the Father, Jesus' relationship with the Spirit, the Spirit's relationship to the Father, or the relationship among all three persons. The interweaving of these four kinds of passages and the finding of the coherent implication of all of them stands behind the development of the doctrine of the Trinity in the early church.

After the Spirit comes at Pentecost, these relationships between Father, Son, and Spirit receive an additional explanation through-

---

10. For a discussion of the biblical materials indicating the unique personhood of the Spirit, see Wainwright, *The Trinity in the New Testament*, 200–4.

out the rest of the New Testament. The apostles have significant insight about who God is from their time with Jesus, but their comprehension increases after Pentecost as the Spirit directs their thinking. When Jesus alerts them that the Spirit will guide them into all truth, surely he intends this to include the truth about the triune nature of God (John 14:26; 16:13). Now, their interpretation of both the life of Jesus and the nature of God provides a much fuller understanding about the divine nature of each of the three members. This oneness of divine essence can be seen in the common way in which they describe the names, attributes, works, roles, and worship of all three members. The conclusion of all of the data from these four kinds of passages may be summed up in four statements:

The Father is God.
Jesus is God.
The Spirit is God.
God is one.[11]

The Trinitarian Structure of the New Testament Books

The first proposal for managing the New Testament materials related to broadening the structure to include references to any two persons of the Trinity. The second proposal has to do with the Trinitarian structure of many New Testament books.

Here the key for discerning how Trinitarian thinking influences the whole New Testament is to observe how many Trinitarian references bracket individual books. Several begin and end with references to all three persons of the Trinity: Matthew (1:20–23; 28:19), Luke (1:35; 24:49), John (1:32–34; 20:21–22); Acts (1:3–5, 7–8; 28:23, 25), Romans (1:1–4; 15:30), 2 Corinthians (1:21–22; 13:14), 1 Thessalonians (1:3–5; 5:18–19), and Revelation (1:4–6; 22:17–18).

The data get stronger if passages that relate two members of the Trinity are included. Even in those books where all three persons of

---

11. Oden, *Living God*, 194ff.

HOLY LOVE: A WESLEYAN SYSTEMATIC THEOLOGY

the Trinity are named at the beginning or the end, the other reference (beginning or end) includes only two members: Mark (1:10–11; 16:19); 1 Corinthians (2:1–4; 15:57); 1 Peter (1:2; 5:10); and Jude (1, 20–21). Still other books make reference to only two members of the Trinity at both the beginning and the end: Galatians (1:3; 6:7–8, 16–17), Ephesians (1:3; 6:23), Philippians (1:2; 4:19–20), Colossians (1:2; 4:12), 2 Thessalonians (1:2; 3:5), 1 Timothy (1:2; 6:14–15), 2 Timothy (1:2; 4:1), Titus (1:4; 3:4–6), Hebrews (1:1–2; 13:20), 1 John (1:3; 5:20), and 2 John (3, 9). Three books open with a reference to two persons of the Trinity: Philemon (1:3), James (1:1), and 2 Peter (1:2). Only 3 John refers to God without specifically naming the Father, the Son, or the Spirit. Second Peter 1:2 reads, "May grace and peace be multiplied to you in the knowledge of God and of Jesus our Lord" (ESV).

Such references are particularly significant if we treat introductions and conclusions as more than formalities. If in fact we are introducing elements that establish a theological context for the book, then Trinitarian references set the stage for an understanding of all this material in light of the persons of the Godhead. In other words the reader is alerted that a new way of understanding God is profoundly shaping the discussion.

The literary structure strengthens this conviction. The principle of *inclusio* dictates that the material enclosed between beginning and ending passages must be interpreted through the lens of those passages—in this case, the Trinitarian references. Matthew is an excellent illustration (Matt. 1:20–23, 28:19). This book comes first in the New Testament, thereby setting the stage for the view of God that is going to be developed thereafter.

Consideration of another literary structure may also assist us: the Law of Generalization and Particularization. These opening statements about the Trinity (either two- or three-person references) give the reader a general statement about the Godhead and then leads one to expect particulars (that is, further details or explanation). The closing statements, on the other hand, interpret enclosed material. The literary method greatly increases the theological significance of the material thus included and demonstrates how pervasive this implicit Trinitarianism was for the thinking of the New Testament church. The Gospel of John and the book of Romans are good illustrations of how this principle of generalizatio n/particularization works.[12]

In sum, if introductions and conclusions help set the stage theologically for books in the New Testament, then the Trinitarian framework for New Testament thinking is extensive. Because the triune God is understood by the early church when only two members of the Trinity are named, the body of Trinitarian data is hugely expanded. An analysis of structure, then, supports the view that all three persons of the Trinity are divine; they share the nature of the Godhead even when writers do not express this in the immediate context. This underlying presupposition governs the early Christian proclamation of the gospel and shapes their own spiritual lives in relationship to the triune God they worship.

TRIUNE LIFE REVEALED IN THE MAKING OF DISCIPLES

A third proposal relates to the organization of Trinitarian passages that do speak of all three persons.[13] The key lies in the theology behind Jesus' central command to make disciples (Matt. 28:19–20).[14] In the final resurrection appearance mentioned

---

12. For a discussion of the literary laws of structure see Traina, *Methodical Bible Study* (New York: Ganis and Harris, 1952), 49–59.

13. Robert Jenson believes that behind the passages that have a threefold reference to the triune God there is a full Trinitarian logic at work. This means that even when the triune formula or triadic form are not used, the logic of talking about God in relationship to Father, Son, and Spirit is compelling enough to force the biblical authors to circle their theme in mentioning how all three persons are included. See *Systematic Theology*, 1:92.

14. For an alternative method of organizing the biblical materials, see T. F. Torrance's use of 2 Cor 13:14 in *The Christian Doctrine of God*, 50–67. For a more traditional listing of major passages used in the early church with reference to all three persons of the Trinity, see the list by Oden of twelve *locus classicus* texts in *The Living God*, 202–8.

HOLY LOVE: A WESLEYAN SYSTEMATIC THEOLOGY

by Matthew, Jesus charges the disciples, "Therefore go and make disciples of all nations, baptizing them in the name of the Father and of the Son and of the Holy Spirit, and teaching them to obey everything I have commanded you" (Matt. 28:18–20). The focus of Jesus' exhortation is to *make disciples*. Only one main verb appears here (i.e., "make disciples") with three participles supplementing the central command ("going," "baptizing," "teaching").[15]

The standard way of using this passage in Trinitarian thinking is to accent the clause, "baptizing them in the name of the Father and of the Son and of the Holy Spirit." Frequently, this is described as a "baptismal formula."[16] Unfortunately, this approach obscures the fact that this reference to the triune God is a part of something much broader than baptism. The issue is exacerbated when what is being symbolized by baptism (a beginning relationship with the triune God) is replaced with the symbol (baptism). So, the ritual act of baptism itself becomes the primary focus instead of the personal relationship with God. Even more problematic is the tendency to associate baptism with public worship events. In this case, the focus centers on a sacramental moment instead of the entire life of believers.

A much more adequate understanding of the role of baptism is to see it as the initial act of making disciples of Jesus. Baptism serves as the beginning of a relationship when people are publicly committed to the name (read "nature") of the triune God. Those who want to be disciples of Jesus must understand that he is connecting them with both the Father and the Spirit as well as himself so that their commitment to Jesus involves a commitment to all three. With this approach we understand that baptism focuses primarily on a beginning relationship with the triune God and that this is the first step in becoming a disciple. The key ingredient is not so

---

15. Coleman, *The Master Plan of Evangelism*, 108–9.
16. Oden, *The Living God*, 202; Fortman, *The Triune God*, 15.

much the formality of a sacrament but the establishment of a relationship with God.[17]

Baptism serves as a symbol that an initial relationship has been established and, like all person-to-person relationships, must be developed. The second half of the Great Commission moves the relationship forward: "teaching them to observe all that I have commanded you" (Matt. 28:20 ESV). This relationship with all three persons of the Trinity progresses in much the same way as Jesus' disciples grew in their relationship with him.[18]

So the Great Commission is not primarily about the formal act of baptizing.[19] Neither is it merely a passage of Scripture that informs the church about its responsibilities in evangelism and missions. It implies the way people learn to relate to God. It begins with an understanding of who God is (triune) and then wraps our relationship with him within becoming disciples of Jesus. From this point on, therefore, to be a disciple of Jesus is to be a disciple of the triune God.

In training his own disciples, Jesus certainly intends that they have some basic knowledge about himself and through him about the Father and the Spirit. So when they are sent to make other disciples, a Trinitarian structure is provided for what he expects them to know. One of the ways to pinpoint the things Jesus wants new disciples to understand is to examine the applicable Trinitarian passages throughout the New Testament.[20]

---

17. Baptism will be treated in part ten, *Ecclesiology*, in volume five of this series.

18. For more on the great commission as the center of the new Jesus movement in both outreach and training, see Coppedge, *Biblical Principles of Discipleship*, 114–18.

19. Cf. Pannenberg's conviction that Matthew 28:19 is not primarily about baptism but about catechizing, i.e., in the development of the Church's teaching the Trinitarian nature of God was to be central (Pannenberg, *Systematic Theology*, 1:268).

20. Accordingly, we have arranged an outline of the passages that refer to all three persons of the Trinity in such a way as to indicate how these teachings shape the thinking of new disciples.

If our analysis is correct, we now have a Trinitarian context both for being a disciple and for making disciples of Jesus. The New Testament data explains the Trinitarian foundation for following Christ. In particular, this material makes clear the nature of the God with whom believers identify at their baptism. This presuppositional mindset established the way the thinkers of the early church thought about themselves in relationship to God, to each other, and to the world. No wonder the church did not settle until it was able to formulate more explicitly the widespread understanding of the nature of this triune God in the New Testament.[21]

---

21. Kelly describes it this way: "If the Trinitarian creeds are rare, the Trinitarian pattern which was to dominate all later creeds was already part and parcel of the Christian tradition of doctrine" (Kelly, *Early Christian Creeds*, 23).

CHAPTER ONE

Old Testament Preparation for the Trinity

THE TRINITARIAN UNVEILING IN the incarnation and Pentecost revealed to the disciples and to the world the nature of the God of Israel. The Old Testament had prepared the way for this self-expression in the promised new covenant and in the triune distinction within the oneness of God.

THE PROMISES OF A NEW COVENANT PREPARE THE WAY FOR A TRIUNE THEISM

In God's promise of the new covenant, he disclosed a way for his people to become like himself, fulfilling his purposes for their lives. God alone established the means whereby the new covenant could be realized. The redemptive plan involves three central components. First, he promises the coming Messiah. Second, the Messiah will minister in the Spirit of God: "The Spirit of the LORD will rest on him" (Isa. 11:2). Third, God himself will come and dwell among his people. Each of these helps prepare the way for a New Testament understanding of the triune God.

First, the promise of the new covenant is closely connected to God's sending of the Messiah to accomplish his purposes among his people and in the world (Isa. 32:1; 42:1; 61:1–4; 11:1–2; Ezek. 36,

37, 39). Whether the coming Messiah is described as servant, king, shepherd, prince, or branch, the Old Testament prophets saw the Messiah as the fulfillment of the new covenant (Ezek. 37:24–26).

Second, many Old Testament passages that describe the coming of the Messiah also indicate that the Spirit will be a part of the Messiah's work (see Isa. 11:1–2; Ezek. 36:14; cf. 39:25–29). In fact, the New Testament portrays the Spirit as playing a pivotal role in the life of Jesus as the promised Messiah (Matt. 1:18, 20; Isa. 9:1–7; 11:2–3). John the Baptist prepares the way for the coming of Jesus as the expected Messiah by declaring that Jesus will baptize them with the Spirit (Matt. 3:11; Mark 1:8; Luke 3:16, John 1:33; Acts 11:16). These new covenant promises begin their fulfillment at the baptism of Jesus. There, not only does the Father speak a word of witness to his Son but also the Spirit comes upon Jesus in a visible way to inaugurate the beginning of his ministry (Matt. 3:16; Mark 1:10; Luke 3:22, 4:1; John 1:32). This baptism fulfills God's promises of a Spirit-filled Messiah (Isa. 11:2–3; 42:1–4).

Finally, the biblical witness deliberately connects Jesus with the Father (the "Holy One of Israel"). While God promises his Spirit and his Messiah in Ezekiel 37, he also promises to come himself: "My dwelling place will be with them; I will be their God, and they will be my people" (Ezek. 37:27). The weaving of these three together—the Messiah, the Spirit, and the Holy One—occurs right after the baptism of Jesus when the Spirit comes upon him and he is thrust out into ministry (Mark 1:24; Luke 4:34).

PLURALITY WITHIN UNITY

One of the Old Testament's major theological battles was for Israel's unique monotheism, but that faith did not rule out distinctions within the unity of God. The primary weapon in the intellectual and spiritual warfare was the Hebrews' constant reiteration of the great Shema: "Hear, O Israel: The LORD our God, the LORD is one" (Deut. 6:4). In the polytheistic world of the ancient Near East, God chose to reveal his oneness to Israel in a definite way. This initiated the most significant intellectual revolution in human history before the incarnation. When Israel's polytheistic neighbors were preoccupied with balancing god against god, Israel's faith rested in the one God who created the world. All they needed for life in the world was found in him. Yet when this God comes into the world he has created and makes himself known in it, he is seen to possess a plurality within himself.[1]

GOD AS FATHER

The earliest references to God as a father are indirect, referring to him as one who has children. Thus, God instructs Moses, "Say to Pharaoh, 'This is what the LORD says: Israel is my firstborn son, and I told you, "Let my son go, so he may worship me." But you refused to let him go; so I will kill your firstborn son'" (Ex. 4:22–23; cf. Isa. 1:2, 4). God is also compared to a father who corrects his son: "As a man disciplines his son, the LORD your God disciplines you" (Deut. 8:5 ESV). The first explicit reference to God as Father comes in the Song of Moses: "Is not he your father, who created you, who made you and established you?" (Deut. 32:6; see Ps. 68:5; 89:26–27; 103:1, 13).

The prophets also speak of God as a loving father. Isaiah records the cry of God's people: "For thou art our Father, though Abraham does not know us and Israel does not acknowledge us; thou, O LORD, art our Father" (Isa. 63:16; 64:8; Jer. 3:19, 22). While Israel was faithless in responding properly to God as a father, he continues to fulfill this role in the restoration of his people. "With supplications I will lead them. . . .For I am a Father to Israel, And Ephraim is My firstborn" (Jer. 31:9; see vv. 20, 22). This familial figure of speech is also used in the wisdom literature. In Proverbs we read, "For the

---

1. For an excellent assessment of the possibility of plurality within monotheism see Bauckham, *God Crucified*.

HOLY LOVE: A WESLEYAN SYSTEMATIC THEOLOGY

LORD reproves him whom he loves, as a father the son in whom he delights" (Prov. 3:12 ESV).[2]

Until the time of David, the references to God as Father in the history of Israel were limited to his role as father of the nation (e.g., Ex. 4:22–23). With the establishment of the monarchy, however, God becomes the father of the king in a special way. David cries unto God, "Thou art my father, my God" (Ps. 89:26–27 KJV; cf. 2 Sam. 7:14). Here, God is not only the father of a nation but the father of an individual.

The Old Testament directly introduces familial language describing God's relationship to his people. When God is described as father in Israel or the king is described as his son, the sharing of life in a close relationship is stressed. So the language of shared life is necessary for gaining an adequate understanding of Jewish monotheism.[3]

THE SPIRIT OF GOD

The Hebrew word for spirit, rûah, may be translated "spirit," "breath," or "wind." Wind aptly symbolizes the power of the work of the Spirit (see Acts 2:2). The concept of breath is a very early connotation of God's Spirit. When God created Adam out of the dust, he "breathed into his nostrils the breath of life . . ." (Gen. 2:7). This may well be a double reference not only to the breath of life but also the Spirit of God. Breath cannot exist without being a part of something else, yet it may be distinguished from the person. So the very nature of the term suggests why it has been chosen to express the idea of "Spirit." This distinction between God and rûah is seen in its first use in Scripture where God creates the heavens and the earth and then the Spirit of God moves over the face of the waters (Gen. 1:1–2).

---

2. See Knight, *A Christian Theology of the Old Testament*, 169–74; cf. Coppedge, *Portraits of God*, 252–57.

3. For the theological implications of God as Father in the Old Testament, see Kasper, *The God of Jesus Christ*, 130–40.

The work of the Spirit in relation to people in the Old Testament is described with various phrases: "Having the Spirit of God," "filled" with the Spirit of God, and other occasions where the Spirit "comes upon them." All describe how God through his Spirit guides a person's life. The two most prominent groups of people upon whom the Spirit of God rests are leaders and prophets. Significantly, these figures seem to be controlled sometimes by God and sometimes by his Spirit (e.g., David in 1 Sam. 16:13, 18). Do the references to God speaking through them or the Spirit of God speaking through them indicate that a plurality in God is being intimated?[4]

One prerogative of deity is to give life. The Spirit of God is certainly connected with this responsibility not only in Genesis 1 and 2, but elsewhere. "The Spirit of God has made me; the breath of the Almighty gives me life" (Job 33:4). While the Spirit comes upon leaders, he also is to be distinguished from God's working in their lives (Num. 11:29).

God himself speaks of sending the Spirit upon other leaders (Joshua in Num. 27:18; Othniel in Judg. 3:9–10; Gideon in Judg. 6:34, 36; Jephthah in Judg. 11:27–29; Samson in Judg. 13:24–25; Saul in 1 Sam. 10:6–7; and David in 1 Sam. 16:12–13). The prophets also distinguish between the Lord speaking to them and the Spirit of God upon them enabling them to speak for God (Balaam in Num. 24:1–2; Azariah in 2 Chron. 15:1–2; Jahaziel in 2 Chron. 20:13–14; Zechariah in 2 Chron. 24:20; Micah in Mic. 7–8; and Daniel in Dan. 5:14, 17–18). This distinction is very clear in the life of Ezekiel when God speaks to the prophet and then sends his Spirit into him (Ezek. 2:1–2; 11:15). In these cases, God's Spirit is distinguished from God.[5]

The early church found three passages in the Old Testament that indicate not only a distinction between God and his Spirit but

---

4. Coppedge, *Holy Living: Godliness in the Old Testament*, unpublished ms, 336–37.
5. For theological evaluation of the Spirit in the Old Testament, see Jenson, *Systematic Theology*, 1:86–88.

perhaps of all three persons of the Trinity. The most impressive of these is Isaiah 48:16, where the promised Messiah is speaking: "'Draw near to me, hear this: from the beginning I have not spoken in secret, from the time it came to be I have been there.' And now the LORD God has sent me, and his Spirit" (ESV). The Lord God (Yahweh Elohim) has sent the Messiah ("me"), but both are distinguished from the Spirit of God. The early church certainly understood this as a veiled reference to Trinitarian thinking.

The second passage is Haggai 2:4–7. Yahweh says, "My spirit abides among you; do not fear. For thus says the Lord of hosts . . . I will shake all the nations, so that the treasure of all nations will come" (Hag. 2:5b–7a NRSVUE). Here the Lord of hosts is clearly distinguished from his Spirit, although both abide with his people. Some have suggested that "the treasure of all nations" (v. 7) refers to the Messiah. Whether or not all three persons are included, Haggai certainly distinguishes Yahweh from the Spirit.

The third reference is Isaiah 61:1. There, the Messiah describes the Spirit of the Lord God as anointing him for the multifaceted work of God. Luke identifies the fulfillment of this passage with the beginning of Jesus' ministry in Nazareth (Luke 4:18).

In all three references, a clear distinction between the Messiah, the Spirit, and the Lord God (Yahweh) is found.[6]

THE WORD OF GOD

The concept of the Word of God is particularly helpful in revealing both the unity and diversity in God. The words a person utters are distinct from the person, yet they are also an extension of who the person is. Thus the "Word of the Lord" in the Old Testament is God speaking, but sometimes this word appears to have an existence of its own. When the Ten Commandments (Ten Words) are given (Ex. 20), the words of God become an extension of God and

---

6. On the Spirit as indicator of the triune God in the Old Testament see Oswalt, "The God of Abraham, Isaac and Jacob" in *The Trinity*, 21–30; see also Wood, *The Spirit of God in the Old Testament*.

represent his presence among his people. The word brings revelation from God, but it also symbolizes God who is still speaking.

The word is also important because it is a symbol of what it means to be a person. It is persons, not things or animals, who understand and speak words. So every time God speaks, there is an accent on his personal nature. Personhood includes rational and verbal capacities for both God and humans. Thus as Samuel grew, "The LORD was with Samuel . . . for the LORD revealed himself to Samuel at Shiloh by the word of the LORD" (1 Sam. 3:19–21 ESV). The Lord's being with Samuel and the Word being with him are closely related, but nevertheless, the two are distinguished. Elsewhere we find that the word of the Lord can be trusted (Ps. 19:42) as the source of life (Ps. 119:25), light (Ps. 119:105), and understanding (Ps. 119:169).[7]

References to the word of God, so pervasive in the Old Testament, prepare the way for people to understand something distinct within God himself. This does not mean that there is a full-blown concept of person, of the word explicit in the Old Testament, but it sometimes is used to express a reality that is present, like one person is present with another (2 Kgs. 3:12). In these cases it seems to be an active subject very similar to the angel or face of Yahweh.[8]

This distinction is more fully developed in the New Testament. John, for example, identifies Jesus as both the Word of God and the one who was with God (John 1:1). He then uses *Word* to show both a unity and diversity in God.

THE WISDOM OF GOD

Wisdom in its proper sense belongs to God alone (Job 12:13; Isa. 31:2; Dan. 2:22–23). His wisdom is particularly related to the practical dimensions of knowledge. Certain things are pro-

---

7. A possible connection between the Word of God and the Second Person of the Trinity is seen right after the description of the great Messianic passage in Isaiah 9:2–8.

8. On the Word and the Spirit see Bobrinskoy, *The Mystery of the Trinity*, 21–36; Hill, *The Three-Personned God*, 5.

duced by God's created wisdom: the universe (Prov. 3:19–20; 8:22–31; Jer. 10:12) and human persons (Job 10:8–12; Ps. 104:24; Prov. 14:31; 22:2). Wisdom, like a word, is related to understanding, counsel, and knowledge, particularly focusing on a practical understanding of truth, reality, and the world.

In terms of wisdom providing veiled intimations of plurality in God, Isaiah connects it with both the Spirit of the Lord upon the Messiah as well as the Spirit of Wisdom (Isa. 11:2). Personification of wisdom in Proverbs (1:20–23; 8:1–36; 9:1–6) led many in the early church to identify the wisdom of God as a separate entity within God himself. The controversial nature of this interpretation was accented when the Arians used the same passages to talk about the creation of wisdom as evidence that Christ was created (Prov. 8:22). Although the early church may have overstated their case about wisdom as a separate person when viewed parallel to the Word of God, it may suggest within itself a plurality, even though its chief expressions probably should be understood in terms of personification rather than a separate hypostasis.[9]

THE ANGEL OF YAHWEH

The "angel of the Lord" (mal'āk YHWH) at first appears as a messenger or representative of Yahweh. The tantalizing part of this data is that sometimes the angel of Yahweh and Yahweh himself seem interchangeable. So, for example, the angel of the Lord appears to Moses in a flame of fire, but then, "When the LORD saw that he turned aside to see, God called to him out of the bush . . ." (Ex. 3:4 ESV). The angel speaks twice to Hagar but is distinguished from the Lord. Yet Hagar concludes the encounter by saying, "Have I even seen Him here and lived after He saw me?" (Gen. 16:13 NASB; cf. Gen. 21:17–19).

This same phenomenon is repeated on multiple occasions (Gen. 16:7; 21:17–19; 22:11–12, 15–16). Sometimes the angel

---

9. For the possible connections of wisdom with Christ or the Spirit, see Bobrinskoy, *The Mystery of the Trinity*, 38–51.

appears to be speaking as God and yet sometimes is clearly distinct from God. We see this in the story of his relationship to Jacob (Gen. 31:11 and 48:15–16), Moses (Ex. 2–6), Balaam (Num. 22:31–35), Israel (Ex. 14:19; 23:20–21; 32:34–33:14; Judg. 1:4), Gideon (Judg. 6:11–23), Manoa and his wife (Judg. 13:3–22), and Zechariah (Zech. 1:1–6:8).

This close identification of Yahweh with the angel of the Lord suggested to many in the early church that the angel might be a preincarnate appearance of the Second Person of the Trinity. The angel of the Lord is closely identified with God (Judg. 6:14; 13:21–22) and at the same time distinguishable from God. God refers to the angel (Ex. 23:23; 32–34) and speaks to him (2 Sam. 24:16; 1 Chron. 21:27), and the angel also speaks to the Lord (Zech. 1:12).

So it seems legitimate to regard the angel of the Lord as a hint of plurality within God. Patristic, medieval, and Reformation commentaries on these passages (using the order of being) identify these references to the angel as preincarnate references to the Second Person of the Trinity. It should be noted, however, that the New Testament does not explicitly identify the Son of God with the angel of the Lord.

A Man of God

Closely related to the angel of the Lord are three places where God is explicitly making himself known, and he is simply called "a man." Although this man is not referred to as the angel of the Lord, many believe such passages are additional references to the angel.

This phenomenon first appears is in the story of Jacob wrestling with a "man" until daybreak (Gen. 32:24–30). The evidence that Jacob is wrestling with God himself is that God refuses to give him his own name, but God blesses him, and Jacob goes away convinced "I saw God face to face . . ." (Gen. 32:30).

The second occurrence comes just as Joshua is ready to lead Israel in the conquest of Canaan. He meets "a man" with his sword drawn. Joshua falls to the earth, worships him, and is instructed to take off his shoes, "for the place where you are standing is holy" (Josh. 5:15). This statement is identical to that given in Moses' encounter with God on Mount Sinai (Ex. 3:5). Joshua's response is appropriate only to deity: worship and full submission.

The third place this "man" appears is in the vision of a new temple God gives Ezekiel. A man appeared to him like bronze, bringing a vision and the measurements and dimension of a new temple (Ezek. 40–42). When Ezekiel falls down to worship, the Spirit of God lifts him up so that he may behold the glory of the Lord filling the temple. Finally, with the man still standing beside him, Ezekiel hears God speak to him out of the temple (Ezek. 43:1–6). If the "man" is in fact a preincarnate appearance of the Second Person of the Trinity, then this is a very Trinitarian manifestation of God's return to his temple.

In all three of these places where a "man" of God appears, there is a clear manifestation of God through him. Whether or not this man is identified with the angel of the Lord, his appearance strongly suggests a preincarnate revelation of the Second Person of the Trinity.[10]

OTHER INTIMATIONS OF PLURALITY

THEOPHANIES

While the appearance of God in human form by itself would not be significant evidence for a plurality within God (e.g., Gen. 32:24–30), God's coming to Abraham as three men is certainly suggestive (Gen. 18). The text says, "the LORD appeared to him" but Abraham beheld, "three men were standing in front of him" (Gen. 18:1–2 ESV). It is possible that Yahweh appears with two angels, but the interchange between "the men" and "the LORD" is a very strong suggestion that the Lord manifests himself visually in a threefold way (Gen. 18:16–17). When the story shifts to Lot in Sodom, the men are described as two angels (Gen. 19).

---

10. Oswalt, "The God of Abraham," 25–27.

A Dialogue Between God and His Son

The messianic Psalm 2 is about the Lord and his anointed (v. 2). The Messiah describes the decree of Yahweh, "He said to me, 'You are my Son, today I have become your father'" (Ps. 2:7–8). Here the Messiah is described as the Son of God, begotten of God, who is in conversation with Yahweh (v. 6). The New Testament writers, looking back on this passage, certainly interpreted it as the Father conversing with the Son (Acts 13:33; Heb. 1:5).

Repetition of the Divine Name

Because the name of God is an alternative way of describing his own personal being, it always carries particular significance in the Old Testament. The adjective most closely associated with the name of God is "holy." So, when Isaiah sees the seraphim calling out to God in a threefold way, it is significant: "Holy, holy, holy, is the LORD of Hosts" (Isa. 6:3). Does a threefold reference to God as holy carry significance other than the accent upon holiness as the essence of his character? It may be the Hebrew way of using the superlative to accent God's holiness. However, the early church viewed this as an intimation of the triunity of God in part because of the similar vision at the end of the New Testament, where the seraphim cry, "Holy, holy, holy is the Lord God Almighty . . ." (Rev. 4:8). The Trinitarian references that surround the vision in Revelation (Rev. 1–4) reinforce their conclusion.

The same could be said about the Aaronic blessing in which the priests pronounced "the name" of God in blessing over his people:

> [Yahweh] bless you and keep you; [Yahweh] make His face
> shine upon you, and be gracious to you; [Yahweh] lift up
> His countenance upon you, and give you peace. So shall
> they put My name on the children of Israel, and I will bless
> them. (Num. 6:24–27 NKJV)

Is the threefold reference to the Lord just a reminder that God is doing all of these things, or does it suggest that God has a threefold nature? Israel understood it the first way, but practical exegetes throughout church history have seen this as one more hint about God's nature that would be fully revealed at a later time.

THE PLURALITY OF THE DIVINE NAME

The chief Hebrew word for God in the Old Testament is *Elohim*, which is plural. This plurality is a little unusual in light of a strong declaration of monotheism within Israel (Deut. 4:6) and is usually explained in terms of a quantitative plural, a plural of intensity or a plural of majesty. Most contemporary scholars opt for a plural of majesty because the word is most often used with a singular verb (e.g., Gen. 1:1). While this certainly may have been the understanding of many in the Old Testament, the possibility of Elohim suggesting something more about the plurality of God is enhanced with the observation that sometimes God speaks with a plural of deliberation: God expresses his decisions with a plural verb.

- God [Elohim] said, "Let us make mankind in our image, in our likeness . . ." (Gen. 1:26).
- The LORD God [Yahweh Elohim] said, "The man has now become like one of us, knowing good and evil. . ." (Gen. 3:22).
- The LORD [Yahweh] said, . . . "Come, let us go down and confuse their language . . ." (Gen. 11:6–7).
- I heard the voice of the LORD saying, "Whom shall I send? And who will go for us? . . ." (Isa. 6:8).

It is certainly not difficult to see why the exegetes of the patristic, medieval, and Reformation periods, trying to think in holistic Trinitarian categories, saw verses such as these as hinting at the triunity in God. Their conviction was, whether or not Elohim or the plural verbs are clear indications of the Trinity, Christians certainly know that the Creator is a triune God.[11]

CONCLUSION

Our review of the Old Testament materials indicates that there are a number of ways that a monotheistic God reveals plurality within his own nature. These include the introduction of God as Father, the Spirit of God, the word of God, the wisdom of God, the angel of the Lord, and the man of God. The strong evidence in all of these cases prefigures a Trinitarian understanding of God. In addition, several other suggestions of plurality, while not as extensive or as compelling, are still important. These include the appearance of God in certain theophanies, the dialogue between God and his Son in Psalm 2, the repetition of the divine name, and the plural character of the name *Elohim*.

This Old Testament data needs to be seen in light of the further revelation of the New Testament.[12] Reading the Old Testament materials in chronological order provides a progressive understanding of a plurality within the nature of the one God. But when read in light of the totality of Scripture, this fuller picture of God allows us to see what was implicit at an earlier stage.[13] While it is necessary to avoid reading too much into the earlier text, we also must be careful to avoid the equally serious error of losing significant dimensions of meaning by neglecting to read it as part of a holistic revelation.[14]

The totality of the biblical data makes it obvious that the concept of a triune God is not related to a few isolated texts. Nor is the concept of a triune God an extracanonical way of thinking. Its

---

11. R. A. Johnson understands the plurality of *Elohim* as a part of a larger concept he feels the Hebrews had of "extension of personality" or "collective personality" (*The One and the Many in the Israelite Conception of God*, 20, cited in Wainwright, *The Trinity in the New Testament*, 20, 23–29).

12. For relation of Old Testament materials to New Testament and both to theological formation see Coppedge, *The God Who Is Triune*, Chapter Two.

13. Ralph del Colle describes this biblical presentation as "primary Trinitarianism" in "Christian Doctrine of God," *The Cambridge Companion to Christian Doctrine*, 123.

14. Oden, *The Living God*, 189, 209.

HOLY LOVE: A WESLEYAN SYSTEMATIC THEOLOGY

widespread base in Scripture inevitably demands that the thinking about God implicit in the Old and New Testaments should be made more explicit as the church lives with the totality of this revelation and its implications.[15]

---

15. Oden describes this correlation of biblical texts as the principle of the analogy of faith, by which one passage of Scripture is understood in relationship to what is known of other passages (*The Living God*, 192).

CHAPTER TWO

The Development of the Doctrine of the Trinity

HAVING SURVEYED THE BIBLICAL foundations of the doctrine of the Trinity, we now move to its historical/theological development. One major purpose for this historical review is to identify the key terms developed by the church to describe Trinitarian reality. These terms are foundational for understanding how the Trinity affects the larger scope of the doctrine of God.

MOTIVATION FOR ARTICULATING THE DOCTRINE OF THE TRINITY

HISTORICAL CONTEXT

As the church faced a variety of practical circumstances in ministry to people, it had to articulate more specifically the truths seen in Scripture. This was particularly important when nonscriptural views (i.e., heresy) began to have a negative impact on the life and ministry of the church. By the time the church came to the general Councils of Nicaea (AD 325) and Constantinople (AD 381), the leaders had been given an opportunity to digest the biblical materials about the triune God and to formulate them in such a way as to refute heresy and to strengthen their spiritual ministry. The church tackled this task so adequately in the fourth century that its doctrinal definition has remained the standard summary of the Trinity for the Christian church across the ages.

Two Key Questions

The two theological issues that demanded an answer from the church were the divinity of Jesus and the divinity of the Holy Spirit. Because the Christian church grew out of a Jewish context, part of its uniqueness in relation to a polytheistic world was its monotheism. Committed to only one God, how were they to explain the incarnation? The Gospel stories give evidence that the accounts about Jesus are in some way about a divine Person. While the full implications of this were surely implicit during Jesus' lifetime, his death and resurrection made his position as the divine Son of God even more clear.

A similar phenomenon happened with the fuller work and revelation of the Spirit at Pentecost. Jesus prepared the way for this revelation (e.g., John 14–16), but when the Holy Spirit came in his fullness (Acts 2), the early church saw how the Spirit works and who he is. In descriptions of Jesus and the Spirit, the New Testament affirms their divinity. But how does the divinity of these two fit with the monotheistic presuppositions inherited from Judaism?[1] The issue forced a revision of their understanding of God.

HISTORICAL ISSUES BEHIND THE DOCTRINE OF THE TRINITY

A variety of nonbiblical teachings about Jesus challenged the church to articulate the doctrine of the Trinity.[2] From the time of the New Testament church, Christian thinkers were aware that to

---

1. Wainwright, *The Trinity in the New Testament*, 3–5. "You will be misleading to say that Trinitarian theology is entirely post-biblical" (4–5).

2. This historical section is heavily indebted to the outline of developments by Kelly, *Early Christian Doctrines*.

explain the deity of Jesus and the Spirit in a monotheistic context, they were going to have to balance the oneness of God with the threeness of God. How one speaks about God is shaped by the initial decision to focus on the unity or the diversity within the Godhead.

Trinitarian thinking faces the theological danger of tritheism. Some feared that focusing on three divine persons would move the church back to polytheism (or tritheism). So in certain historical discussions, when too much emphasis was placed on the three persons, this danger signal was raised. Fortunately, throughout most of church history the church's foundation in Old Testament monotheism has prevented it from embracing tritheism. The monotheistic presupposition was so strong that most theological problems arose from too much emphasis on the oneness of God. The theological task has always been to find a balance between unity and diversity in the Godhead because both are thoroughly documented in Scripture.

Historically, three nonbiblical ideas about Jesus have their roots in this overemphasis on the unity of God: adoptionism, modalism, and Arianism. In the most general terms these are all described within the category of monarchianism. "Monarch," in this context, refers to one archē (origin or source), so this designation, monarchianism, accents God's oneness. How did these positions focus on God as the one origin?

ADOPTIONISM

Adoptionism is sometimes referred to as "dynamic monarchianism." Christ was described as the "new man" on whom the Spirit of God descended. Adoptionists do not see Jesus as divine from his conception to his ascension but rather he was "adopted" by the Father at his baptism.

In this view Jesus represents God, but God's *monarchia* is preserved. This theory is often attributed to Theodotus (c. AD 190), whose view was that prior to Jesus' baptism he was not the Son of God but an ordinary man who lived a virtuous life. At his baptism when the Spirit descended upon him, Jesus was adopted as God's Son. Then he began to work miracles—without becoming divine. Others following Theodotus suggested that Jesus was deified at his resurrection.

Paul of Samosatawas another well-known proponent of adoptionist thinking. In the third century he proposed a theory that denied any personality or subsistence to the Word of God. A thinly veiled unitarian, he thought "the Son" and "the Spirit" were merely the church's names for the inspired man Jesus Christ and the grace of God that was poured upon the apostles. The Council of Antioch condemned him in AD 268.[3]

The church opposed adoptionism by pointing out that it focused on only a few texts of Scripture and did not take into account the larger biblical picture. In particular it did not factor in the passages of Scripture that reveal the eternal relationship of Jesus to the Father (e.g., John 1:1–18; Phil. 2:5–11). Nor did it take seriously enough the birth narratives and the incarnation that describe Jesus' divinity before his baptism (e.g., Matt. 1:20–23; Luke 1:35; John 1:1–3; Phil. 2:5–11; Col. 1:15–19; Heb. 1:1–5). So adoptionist Christology was deemed biblically inadequate and unacceptable.[4]

MODALISM

The second form of monarchianism is sometimes called "modalistic monarchianism." Connected with Sabellius of Ptolemais, it is also known as Sabellianism. Modalism so strongly emphasizes the oneness (*monarchia*) of God that the Father, Son, and Spirit were understood as merely three different ways of viewing the same God—like looking at three faces of God as he revealed himself as Father in the Old Testament, as Son in the Gospels, and as the Spirit in Acts. To put it another way, the three persons describe God in

---

3. For references to monarchianism see Kelly, *Early Christian Doctrines,* 115–18; Lonergan, *The Way to Nicea,* 36–37; Oden, *The Living God,* 12; Pelikan, *The Emergence of the Catholic Tradition,* 175–78.

4. Ignatius, "Trallians XI," *ANF,* 1:71; Oden, *Living God,* 212; Kelly, *Early Christian Doctrines,* 115–19.

himself, God revealed, and God active in other persons. The distinctions were real, but they designated human perceptions of God rather than separate persons of the Trinity. For the modalist, God is not three persons; he is one person who plays three different roles. This position so focused on the oneness of God that it failed to adequately distinguish the three divine persons.[5]

The church responded to modalism by showing that this position had not adequately taken into account the biblical data about the distinctness of the persons of the Trinity. Emphasizing the monarchy or oneness of God, the modalists did not take into account the passages of Scripture where *the three persons relate to one another.* Biblical passages indicating a clear distinction of the persons within God include Jesus' communication with the Father before the creation of the world (John 1:1–4) and his ongoing communication with Father while on earth (John 17). Church theologians wondered why the Scripture presented God as talking to himself if in fact the persons of the Trinity are only three facets or modes of God.

The early church was fully aware that God worked in different roles. But they did not believe that the Father, Son, and Spirit were roles that a unitary God played in relation to the world. They did not think that modalism adequately explained the biblical materials describing the distinctions of God.

ARIANISM

The most significant challenge to Trinitarian thought came from a presbyter named Arius, who began to publish his views in Alexandria in AD 318. Beginning with the monarchy of God, his fundamental presupposition was the unique transcendence of a monotheistic God who was the unoriginate source of all reality. Thus Arius shares with dynamic monarchianism (adoptionism) and modalistic monarchianism (modalism) an over-emphasis on the oneness

---

5. Kelly, *Early Christian Doctrines*, 119–23; Oden, *The Living God*, 213; Lonergan, *Way to Nicea*, 38–39; Pelikan, *Emergence of the Catholic Tradition*, 179; Bobrinskoy, *The Mystery of the Trinity*, 217–20.

(*monarchia*) of God. But his way of accounting for the role of Jesus and the Spirit was somewhat different. Beginning with the transcendent and the individual nature of God, he was convinced that the essence (*ousia*) of God could not be shared or communicated to another without undermining monotheism. Therefore, everything (including the Son and the Spirit) other than God must have come into existence by an act of creation. So the heart of his thinking was that Jesus and the Spirit were created beings.

Arian thought may be summarized in four statements. First, the Father created the Son out of nothing by fiat. The use of the term "beget" really means to "make." The Son is not self-existent but is God's perfect creature above all others. Second, the Son must have had a beginning if he was created. The standard Arian description is, "There was when he was not." To allow that the Son was coeternal with the Father undermined the *monarchia* of the Father. Third, because the Son does not share the Father's essence, he has no direct knowledge of or communion with the Father. Jesus may be called the Word and the Wisdom, but he is distinct from the word or wisdom that comes from the Father. He participates in the communication of God's word and wisdom, but he is still a creature, alien from and dissimilar to the Father's essence. Fourth, as a created being, the Son is liable both to change and even to the possibility of sin.

Why then should the Son be called God or the Son of God? The Arians answer that these were courtesy titles.[6] So when Arius speaks of a Holy Triad, he envisions the three as having entirely different essences and not sharing the same basic nature. The effective result is to make the Son a demigod. Even though he transcends other creatures, he is no more than a creature in relationship to the Father. The same things would be said of the Spirit.[7] The Arian explanation of Jesus as a created being is called subordinationism.

6. DeMargerie, *Christian Trinity and History*, 87, 89; Pelikan, *The Emergence of the Catholic Tradition*, 191–200; Lonergan, *The Way to Nicea*, 68–87.

7. Kelly, *Early Christian Doctrines*, 226–30.

Basically they argued that Jesus, and later the Spirit, are subordinate to God the Father in their essence.[8]

The threat of Arianism forced the church to articulate in unambiguous terms the doctrine of the Trinity. The church did not create something new but synthesized all the biblical materials about the person of Jesus, helping Christians comprehend what had bee part of their proclamation since the fourth century through the historic creeds. Because their response to Arianism was so significant in the theological formulation of the doctrine of the Trinity, we now turn our attention to the development of the creeds.

THE CHURCH'S RESPONSE TO INADEQUATE THEOLOGY

SCRIPTURE, THEOLOGY, AND CREED: DEVELOPING CONCEPTUAL TOOLS

The theological issues raised by these historical deviations from apostolic proclamation required the church to spell out what it did and did not believe about the person of Jesus and what this meant for its understanding of God. Just as it had responded to adoptionism and modalism, the church father's response to Arianism was that it used Scripture selectively and did not take into account all the biblical data about the Father, Son, and Spirit. Immersed in Scripture, the early church fathers worked together to develop a holistic understanding of God. The concise version of this was set down at the general Councils of Nicea (AD 325) and of Constantinople (AD 381).

The fruits of their labor is known as the Nicene Creed (or Nicene/Constantinopolitan Creed), which distills essential biblical truths about the persons of the Trinity and their relationship to one another. This creed still serves as a shorthand way to distinguish

---

8. On Arianism as a form of subordinationism, see Prestige, *God in Patristic Thought*, 146–56; T. F. Torrance, *The Christian Doctrine of God*, 13–18.

HOLY LOVE: A WESLEYAN SYSTEMATIC THEOLOGY

the orthodox position of the church from Arianism and other distorted views of God. The creed was designed as a brief summary of essential biblical truth about who Jesus is, and therefore who the Father and the Spirit are. The early church leaders believed they were defending biblical faith against distortion. Therefore, they used more precise language than that found in the New Testament. This exact creedal language made it more difficult for heretical groups to sound biblical while in reality circumventing the heart of biblical truth. The church fathers did not see their work as the invention of new doctrine but as a synthesis of the apostolic teaching from the New Testament that had been proclaimed within the church from the beginning.

The development of the orthodox view of the triune God meant crafting certain intellectual concepts to express what they understood Scripture to be saying. The Nicene Creed holds together the threeness and the oneness of God and thus preserves the biblical data on both. The Nicene Fathers built this into the creed itself by beginning, "We believe in one God." Then the one God is defined as, "the Father Almighty," "One Lord Jesus Christ, the Only begotten Son of God," and, "the Holy Ghost, the Lord and Giver of Life." There is indeed an accent on the oneness of God, but God is defined in terms of three persons.

The threeness of the persons is held together in the oneness of God by means of statements that the Father and the Son are of the same essence (*homoousia*). This language spoke directly to the Arians who thought Jesus was a created being who did not share the same essence with God. *Homoousios* was reinforced by declaring that Jesus is "the only begotten Son of God, begotten of the Father before all worlds, Light of Light, of very God, begotten, not made, being of one substance [*homoousia*] with the Father."[9] This sharing of the same essence was extended to the divine nature of the Holy Spirit. Instead of using the term *homoousios*, however, the

---

9. See T. F. Torrance, *The Christian Doctrine of God*, 80–81.

church fathers describe the Spirit as "the Lord and Giver of Life," an alternative way of making the same point but still a clear indication of the full divinity of the Spirit. The result was that both the Son and the Spirit were given fully divine status in the creed, and the theological term that best describes this is *homoousios*. This language allowed the creedal authors to maintain the oneness of God while at the same time indicating God eternally exists as three different persons.[10]

The next key theological component developed was the historic formula describing the Trinity: *one essence, three persons.* Differentiating the three within the triune God was accomplished by distinguishing the persons according to their relations to one another. So the Father is understood as "unoriginate," the Son as "eternally begotten," and the Spirit as "eternally proceeding" from the Father, through the Son. This distinguished the relations of the persons of the Trinity in terms of the being (i.e., ontology) of the Godhead. The persons of the Trinity can also be distinguished by their functional relationship to creation, describing the Trinity in its relations to God's plan, or *economia*, for the world. Here the Father is more fully identified with the work of creation, the Son with the provision of redemption, and the Spirit with the application and consummation of redemption.

The third key theological tool is the concept of shared existence, which centers around the use of the term *perichoresis* or "coinherence," meaning each person of the Trinity shares fully in the life of the other two; each fully permeates and participates in the existence of the others; each coinheres in the life of the others. As we pursue the full implications of Trinitarian theology, we will find that this term becomes significant at every level of theological discourse: hypostatic union, union with God, and fellowship with other believers.

---

10. For an excellent discussion of the development of the *homoousia* and its theological implications for the doctrine of the Trinity, see Kasper, *The God of Jesus Christ*, 258–63.

These major components—the term *homoousia*; the formula *one essence, three persons*; and the concept of *perichoresis*—made it possible to establish an orthodox doctrine of the Trinity. With these conceptual tools the church felt that it had distilled scriptural truth in a way that was an accurate representation of the New Testament while at the same time making it possible to defend the church against distorted views. While the theologians of the early church made generous use of Greek terms and ideas to articulate the theology of the gospel, they reshaped them in significant ways in light of Scripture. The use of words like "being," "Word," and "act" come to mean something quite different than in Platonic, Aristotelian, or Stoic thought. They are in fact rather "un-Greek." As T. F. Torrance puts it, "Far from Nicene theology resulting from a Hellenization of biblical Christianity, there took place in it a Christian recasting of familiar Hellenistic thought-forms in order to make them vehicles for the saving truth of the Gospel."[11]

In the end, the Nicene Creed became a test of orthodoxy, specifically but not exclusively directed toward the Arian threat.[12] Its wording makes it possible to distinguish competing and unorthodox views about God. It identifies the church's consensual understanding of what the Scripture teaches about God the Father, God the Son, and God the Holy Spirit.[13]

TWO APPROACHES TO THE TRINITY

The branches of the Christian church have tended to approach the Trinity from different directions.[14] Some begin with God's unity and then try to account for the three persons; others begin with the three persons and then accent God's unity. Where one begins

---

11. T. F. Torrance, *The Trinitarian Faith*, 74.

12. For more on the leaders of the early church and how they developed these theological tools, see Coppedge, *The God Who Is Triune*, Chapter Three.

13. Oden, *Living God*, 213–15.

14. Rahner, *The Trinity*, 58ff.

in the process seems to have significant implications for the ultimate outcome.

Historical Development of the Different Approaches to the Trinity

In very general terms the Eastern church, led by Athanasius and the Cappadocians, emphasized the three persons, basing their thinking on the New Testament accounts of the three. They solved the unity problem with the concept of the *homoousios*. The unity of the three persons was made clear through the concept of *perichoresis*, which revealed how the three distinct persons could share the same essence. In their understanding, the economic Trinity revealed in Scripture is continuous with the Ontological Trinity; that is, God in his inner being has the same threeness as in his relations to creation. Thus the approach in the Eastern church helped establish the Nicene-Constantinopolitan understanding of the Trinity.

The Western church, on the other hand, has been influenced more by Augustine's theology of God.[15] His emphasis on the unity and his discomfort with the concept of persons led him to focus more on the one than on the three.[16] Augustine's emphasis on the unity of God was reinforced by Boethius' definition of a person as an "individual substance of a rational nature." Thus, throughout the Middle Ages, thinkers like Aquinas focused on the unity and rationality of God, beginning their theologies with his being and existence. So, since Aquinas, the writing of theology in the West normally begins

---

15. For an overview of Augustine's impact on the Western church, see Jenson, *Triune Identity*, 131–38. See pages 14–121 on the broad general distinctions between the Eastern and Western churches.

16. For the impact of Augustine's Trinitarian approach on spirituality in the West, see Houston, "Spirituality and the Doctrine of the Trinity," in *Christ in Our Place*, 53–87.

HOLY LOVE: A WESLEYAN SYSTEMATIC THEOLOGY

discussing the existence and the being of God before discussing the triune nature of God.[17]

This pattern was followed not only by Roman Catholic scholastics but also by Protestant Reformers. It is also reinforced in contemporary thought through the influence of Descartes, who looked within a single individual to find the basis of his epistemology. Descartes' influence is reflected in Kant and the Enlightenment thinkers who tended to focus on the individual and the intellect in the discussion of God.

In his pioneering work in the twentieth century, Karl Barth reopened the discussion of the Trinity. However, Barth's reluctance to talk about the persons of the Trinity still leads to an accent on the oneness of God. When describing three persons, Barth refers to three "modes of existence." This naturally leads to an understanding of one God in a threefold repetition that Moltmann describes as "nothing other than Christian monotheism."[18] Others who have followed Barth by focusing primarily on the unity of the Trinity include Bernard Lonergan among the Roman Catholics and among the Protestants Emil Brunner, Wayne Grudem, Thomas Oden, Louis Berkhof, John Feinberg, and John Frame.

Alternatively, following Athanasius and the Cappadocian Fathers, some theologians focus on the diversity within the Godhead, placing the accent on the distinction of the three persons.[19] One such figure in the East is Gregory Palamas (1293–1381). But representatives of this viewpoint have not been limited to the East.

---

17. La Cugna, *God for Us,* 43–44, 96–97; Pannenberg, *Systematic Theology,* 1:287–89. Gunton, "Augustine, The Trinity and the Theological Crisis of the West," in *The Promise of Trinitarian Theology,* 31–55; Moltmann, *The Trinity and The Kingdom,* 16–17; For an alternative evaluation of Augustine, see the discussion in Kärkkäinen, *The Doctrine of God,* 79–80; Kasper, *God of Jesus Christ,* 296–97, and Michael Barnes, "Augustine in Contemporary Trinitarian Theology," 237–50.

18. Moltmann, *Trinity and the Kingdom,* 69, 139–44.

19. The first to call attention to this distinction between the East and the West was Theodore de Regnon, *Etudes de Theologie Positive sur la Sainte Trinite,* 1:433.

In the West it is seen clearly in Richard of St. Victor's (d. 1173) significant analogy of interpersonal love.[20] This same perspective may be seen in the work of William of St. Thierry (1085–1148) and Jan van Ruysbroeck (1293–1381).[21] Among those segments of the Western Church with a stronger focus on the role of the Spirit, a clearer understanding of the different roles and distinctness of the Trinity emerges. Some of this appears in John Wesley and John Fletcher as a part of the eighteenth-century revival movement in Britain. Its contemporary form finds expression in the work of Karl Rahner among the Roman Catholics and in Protestantism Jürgen Moltmann and Wolfhart Pannenberg.[22] The latter are students of Karl Barth, but they pay more attention to the persons of the Trinity and not just the monarchy of God. Still later expressions of this revived interest come from T. F. Torrance (Church of Scotland), John Zizioulas (Orthodox), Walter Kasper and Catherine LaCugna (Roman Catholic), Colin Gunton (United Reformed Church), and Robert Jenson (Lutheran).[23]

The churches related to Eastern Orthodoxy generally take this approach to the Trinity, and in the West some free churches (as opposed to state churches) have begun to be open to the working of the Spirit, which comes out of a greater understanding of persons of the Trinity. Where voluntary societies within larger churches appear, the same tendency may be detected.[24]

---

20. See Pannenberg's evaluation of the positive contribution of Richard in *Systematic Theology*, 1:286–87.

21. William of St. Thierry, *The Enigma of Faith*; Ruysbroeck, *The Spiritual Espousals*; and Dupré, *The Common Life*.

22. In spite of Rahner's fresh emphasis on the threeness of God, Moltmann identifies his view as very similar to that of Barth and refers to it as Rahner's idealistic modalism, which he feels is only another form of Christian monotheism (Moltmann, *Trinity and the Kingdom*, 144–48).

23. See Jenson's call for correction of the Western tradition's dysfunctional use of the doctrine of the Trinity in both piety and theology in *Systematic Theology*, 1:110–14.

24. For an alternative evaluation of this difference of approach between East and West, see Hart, *The Beauty of the Infinite*, 169–75.

While drawing a distinction between those who begin with the unity of the Trinity and those who begin with the persons of the Trinity carries the risk of painting with too broad a brush, there are some indicators that the contemporary church reflects the two different approaches. And, of course, each approach seems to entail certain theological and practical implications.[25]

---

25. Gunton, *The Promise of Trinitarian Theology*, 31–57; Kasper, *The God of Jesus Christ*, 261-263; La Cugna, *God for Us*, 21–205. For further evaluation of contemporary interest in the Trinity, see Grenz, *Rediscovering the Triune God.*

CHAPTER THREE

The Triune God in Relation to Creation

CRAFTING THE TERMINOLOGY

AN HISTORICAL REVIEW SHOWS how the discussion of the Trinity was shaped by a refining of language. The Eastern church worked in Greek and the Western church in Latin, which complicated their communication and the clarification of terms. In the final analysis, however, the church leaders defined their own terms in the chosen language to carry specific meaning. They did not allow the terms of Greek and Latin metaphysics to determine Christian theology. Rather, the careful theological articulation of early church thinkers reshaped the use of key words in both Greek and Latin—the church influenced the culture rather than vice versa.[1]

By the Fifth Ecumenical Council in Constantinople (AD 553), church leaders were confessing three *hypostases* (or persons) within the one nature (or essence) of the consubstantial Trinity. To phrase it slightly differently, they were committed to three consubstantial subsistences (*hypostases*/persons) in one single divinity or divine

---

1. T. F. Torrance believes this was one of the most significant features of Nicene theology, "not the Hellenizing of Christianity, but the Christianizing of Hellenism" (*The Trinitarian Faith*, 68).

substance (*ousia*/essence).[2] Table 1 shows the English, Greek, and Latin terms in perspective.

Table 1. Key Terms of Trinitarian Theology

ENGLISH	GREEK	LATIN
essence substance	*ousia*	*essentia* *substantia*
person	*hypostasis* *prosopon*	*persona*
same essence consubstantial	*homoousios*	*consubstantia*
coinherence	*perichoresis*	*circuminsessio*
mode of existence of God		*subsistentia in* *divina essentia*
three persons, one essence	three *hypostases*, one *ousia*	three *personae* one *essentia*

TWO APPROACHES TO THE TRINITY

The theological discussion of the Trinity must begin with the recognition that we approach the triune God from two perspectives. One is in terms of how God has made himself known to the created world. From this approach, which is termed the Economic Trinity (economy = plan, order), we know God as revealed through his relationship to creation, particularly in Israel, in the incarnation, and at Pentecost. We come to know the triune God—how God relates to us in our world—through the unfolding story of progressive revelation. Here the Trinity is understood according to function.

But once we understand the working of the economic Trinity, we immediately wonder how the persons relate to each another. This internal relationship of God is called the Ontological Trinity (*ontos* = being), which refers to the inner relationships of three persons within the being of the one God. This may be described as the Trinity understood according to essential nature.

---

2. For the development of the terms *hypostasis* and *ousia* see Prestige, *God in Patristic Thought*, 179–96.

Whether we describe the Trinity in terms of how God relates to the world (*pro nobis*) or how he relates to himself (*in se*), we are relating to the same God. This assumes that there is a coherence between what God does in relationship to the world and in relationship to his own being. This presupposes that what God has revealed about himself through his actions toward creation also gives us an accurate (although not exhaustive) understanding of who he is within himself. Therefore, we must begin with the premise that there is one Trinity and that God is the same in his own inner being as he is in his actions toward us. Different terms have come to be used (Economic Trinity and Ontological Trinity) to describe our different approaches to understanding the triune God. However, we need a regular reminder that we are dealing with one God and that he is the same in his inward being as he is in his outward manifestations.[3]

Having declared our conviction that God is consistent in his action and being, we must also acknowledge that we begin knowing God through the Economic Trinity. The God who made himself known as Yahweh in the Old Testament has unfolded a clearer picture of himself as Father, Son, and Spirit in the New Testament. So the description of God as the Economic Trinity, God making himself known to us in our world, is our key to knowing him. This is what dominates the biblical materials. Once we come to the end of this data, we are in a position to see how all of the evidence fits together to tell us who God is in himself, that is, the Ontological Trinity. This means we infer from the data about God in Scripture what God really is within himself. Once we have the revelation that describes the Economic Trinity, we still have the theological task of articulating what this implies about God in himself. Regarding this, T. F. Torrance says, "what God is toward us in the Word and Activity of Christ and the Spirit he is in his ultimate being or *ousia*."[4]

---

3. T. F. Torrance, *The Christian Doctrine of God*, 7.
4. T. F. Torrance, *The Christian Doctrine of God*, 129.

HOLY LOVE: A WESLEYAN SYSTEMATIC THEOLOGY

This movement from observing what God reveals about himself in Scripture (primarily about the Economic Trinity) to knowing God as he existed before the creation of the world and in himself (the Ontological Trinity) is the shift from the order of knowing (progressive revelation) to the order of being (a holistic view).[5] When we see the unity and coherence of the biblical data, which gives a whole picture of God as he is apart from creation in the order of being, we are in a better position to understand more fully what he was saying via order of knowing. So there is a mutual relationship between the order of knowing and the order of being, each illuminating the other.[6] The parts make possible a knowledge of the whole, and, in turn, the whole illuminates the parts.

The consistency between the Economic Trinity and the Ontological (Immanent) Trinity has been most clearly articulated by Karl Rahner in his famous axiom, "The economic Trinity is the immanent Trinity, and the immanent Trinity is the economic Trinity."[7] This statement is so significant that it is now called "Rahner's Rule."[8] It reminds the church that the God who has made himself known in creation, redemption, and sanctification is not different from who God is in himself.[9]

THE ECONOMIC TRINITY: *OPERA AD EXTRA*

The church has always understood that God unfolds revelation about himself as Father, Son, and Holy Spirit in areas like cre-

---

5. The order of knowing may be described by the phrase *Ordo Congnoscendi* and the order of being with the phrase *Ordo Essendi* (T. F. Torrance, *The Christian Doctrine of God*, 136).

6. For further discussion on the relationship of the order of knowing, or the epistemological order, to the order of being, or the ontological order, see Coffey, *Deus Trinitas*, 15–16.

7. Rahner, *The Trinity*, 22.

8. For discussion of the value and limitations of Rahner's axiom, see Kasper, *The God of Jesus Christ*, 273–77.

9. For a qualified use of Rahner's rule, see Hart, *The Beauty of the Infinite*, 155–75, 179f.

ation, redemption, and sanctification. This is how God relates to our world; these actions are the external operations of the Trinity, captured in the phrase *opera ad extra* ("works of the Trinity on the outside").

The progressive unfolding of this data reveals God's plan, or the economy of God: the Economic Trinity. To avoid the contemporary implications of the term "economic," other terms have been suggested, including: Evangelical Trinity, the Revealed Trinity, or the Operational Trinity. All of the terms have their advantages and disadvantages, but because of its long history, we will continue to use Economic Trinity.

A DIFFERENCE IN THREENESS: DIVERSITY IN REVELATION AND REDEMPTION

Every act of God is Trinitarian, but those acts are distributed in a personal and dynamic way. Scripture indicates that particular members of the Trinity are closely connected with certain activities in relationship to our world. This does not mean that the other members are not also involved, but each of the three has a locus of work and responsibility. This means there is diversity in their functions, but certainly not an absolute division of labor. This diversity relates to two major areas: revelation and redemption.

THE ECONOMIC TRINITY AND REVELATION

The best formula to give us a shorthand résumé of how God works in relation to us in revelation is to describe it as *from the Father through the Son by the Spirit*.

Revelation from the Father focuses on two areas. First, the created world makes it possible for God to speak to his creatures from the physical creation, from reason, from conscience, and from a variety of experiences. These experiences are further subdivided in terms of the physical creation, animals and people, including personal, familial, and social/cultural/political relationships. The fact that the Father is especially connected with creation means that he is speaking to us through the creative order and its various dimensions (see Ps. 19:1–6; Acts 13:24–29; Rom. 1–2).

The Father also speaks to us verbally, and this is seen particularly in his direct speech to Israel and the events by which he made himself known. Through accurate recording and interpretation, the events were translated into words, and thus God's special revelation comes to us first in the Old Testament and then in the New. So God as Father has revealed himself to us through general revelation and special revelation, the second being the control and interpreter of the first.

The Father speaks through the Son, and just as the Father speaks through word and event, so the Son comes to us as both word and event (or model). He is described as the living Word (John 1:1–4), who speaks what is given to him by the Father. His words are the heart of God's communication in the Gospels, and his life modeled or illustrated most things that he verbalized. So there is a match between his life and his speech. His incarnation was a living model of what God wants us to understand, and his words are a more exact description of what God wants us to hear. Both his life and words then become part of God's special revelation to his people.[10]

Though the Father speaks through the Son, he also speaks *by the Spirit*. The Spirit's role in special revelation is to oversee the record of that revelation in Scripture. He is often described as the one who actually is responsible for what God has said in Scripture. But he also witnesses to the hearts of individuals that the Scripture is true. This classic Reformation doctrine declares that the word given by God in Scripture is witnessed to by the Spirit as the truth. So there is a double witness to individuals, externally in Scripture and internally by the Spirit.[11]

---

10. This revelation of God may also be described as coming both by word and by being. It is possible because of the *homoousios*—the identity of the Son with the Father—so that there is a full correlation between what the Father reveals through the Son and what God really is in himself, in his own being. (T. F. Torrance, *The Christian Doctrine of God*, 143).

11. Calvin, *Institutes of the Christian Religion*, 1:85–92.

The Spirit further witnesses to general revelation as interpreted through the lens of Scripture so that the Spirit, in light of special revelation, assists God's people to interpret what God is saying through general revelation in creation, reason, conscience, and experience.

The sum is that God the Father has spoken through the Son and by the Spirit so that all three members of the Trinity are involved in revelation, but each has a slightly different function in this revelatory work. This is true with regard to the total revelation of God to us, but it is particularly true of revelation of the triune God about himself. As T. F. Torrance says, "As God may be known only through himself, through his self-revelation, so the Holy Trinity may be known only through the Trinity, in God's Trinitarian self-revelation of himself."[12]

The presupposition behind this connection between the Economic Trinity and revelation is that God alone makes himself known through the Son and the Spirit. Because of the triune nature of God in revelation, we know that we are getting an accurate description of what God is really like. Thus God is never to be thought of as something different from what he has made known about himself in the person of Jesus and revealed to us by the Spirit. He is exactly as the Son and the Spirit have made him known. This gives us confidence that we can actually know God as he is, not as hidden and obscure but as self-revealing. He has made himself known to us so that we might enter into relationship with him as Father, Son, and Spirit.

The Trinity not only speaks to us in revelation, but God also expects a response from us to his revelation. Again, all three persons of the Trinity are involved. The formula that best helps us understand how this works is that we respond *by the Spirit through the Son to the Father*.[13]

---

12. T. F. Torrance, *The Christian Doctrine of God*, 74.
13. See Pannenberg, *Systematic Theology*, 1:331.

HOLY LOVE: A WESLEYAN SYSTEMATIC THEOLOGY

We respond to God's revelation *by the Spirit*. The Spirit helps us receive revelation both from Scripture and nature. The Spirit opens our spirits so that we can understand and be receptive to the truth; he helps us understand what God is saying. Then the Spirit witnesses to this revelation as truth. Finally, the Spirit empowers us to respond positively to the revelation we have received from God, bringing an enabling grace that allows us to be receptive, to trust, and then to respond appropriately (i.e., obedience, love, and thanksgiving, etc.).

This assistance from God comes by the Spirit *through the Son*. God's revelation concentrates on the person of Jesus, and his primary design is for us to come to know about the Son so that we may actually come to know the Son.

Then the work of God by the Spirit through the Son leads us *to the Father*. This means that the Spirit leads us to the Son, and the Son leads us to the Father (John 14:9). Our response to revelation is not just a passive receptivity but also a positive response that brings us into relationship to all three members of the Trinity. So by the Spirit through the Son we come to know the Father, and in knowing the Father we know the Son and the Spirit.

The Economic Trinity and Redemption

The persons of the Trinity not only relate to the created world in terms of revelation but also in terms of redemption. This refers to what God does in remaking relationships with people.

The Economic Trinity relates to us in redemption *from the Father through the Son by the Spirit*. Each person of the Trinity is particularly identified with some function in the process. The other two members, though, serve in a complementary, perichoretic way.[14]

Redemption begins *from the Father* and is particularly related to the creation of the world according to God's purposes. While

---

14. More contemporary language might describe one member in each function as the "point person."

Scripture clearly indicates that the Son and the Spirit have a part in creation, including God's purposes, the Father seems to be the "representative person" in the biblical picture of how God relates to us. Unfortunately, God's purposes for his people have been interrupted by the entrance of sin (Gen. 3). So God's purpose in redemption is to restore people so they might ultimately reflect his original design for them at creation.

The creation of the universe and of people to reflect God's likeness is accomplished by the Father *through the Son*. Redemption is provided through Jesus' incarnation, life, death, and resurrection. The Second Person of the Trinity is the incarnate one who lives a sinless life and who dies and is raised from the dead to provide for God's redeeming work among people. The Son functions uniquely in redemption; he participates in redemption in a way that neither the Father nor the Spirit do.

The Father is the key person in creating and establishing his purposes for us in the world. The Son is responsible for providing redemption. But the Spirit is primarily responsible for the actualization of this redemption. So the formula is *from the Father through the Son by the Spirit*. The Spirit's work is sometimes described as sanctification, or the application of redemption or the consummation of God's work. The Spirit actually applies the redeeming grace provided through the Son in the individual lives of people. He is the agent of the new birth that begins to regenerate people and make them again like God. The Spirit is also the one who restores human persons to a right relationship with God. So the Spirit is the personal presence of the triune God working in individuals to bring them into a right relationship with the whole Godhead. He is also the one who subjectively transforms people on the basis of the redemption the Son provided so that they then can fulfill God's purposes to be a holy people, reflecting fully the image of the triune God.

God has worked from himself to us to make redemption available, and we respond in a parallel way, captured succinctly in Ephesians 2:18, which speaks of how we relate to God through Jesus in the Spirit: "For through him [the Son] we both have access to the Father by one Spirit."

In redemption the Trinity works in us *by the Spirit through the Son to the Father*. This means that the Spirit draws us to God when we receive his revelation. The Spirit also enables us by grace to respond in faith to the Son. So the work of God the Spirit in us first enables us to receive revelation and then empowers us to respond by faith. By the Spirit we are drawn through faith in the Son to the Father.

This Trinitarian mode of working expresses itself in a variety of ways in our experiences of knowing him and appropriating his grace. In our pre-salvation experience we are drawn by the Spirit through the prevenient grace provided by the Son toward the Father. In salvation the Spirit becomes the agent for the new birth, which brings the Son's saving grace so a relationship is established with the Father, and we are renewed in the image of the triune God.

But God continues to work after our experience of initial redemption. We experience the witness of God's Spirit, who reassures us of the Son's saving grace, which in turn gives us assurance of our relationship to God the Father. This fosters growth in the image and likeness of God (progressive sanctification) by living in the Spirit, and growth in the grace that the Son has provided and in a deepening relationship with the Father (and the whole Godhead). Full sanctification may be described as the infilling of the Spirit, where purification from sin is made possible by the grace of the Son so that one is able to experience the fullness of God and to love unconditionally as the Father does. Then it becomes possible to go on to maturity, in further growth after full sanctification. This consists of walking in the fullness of the Spirit and growing in grace toward mature likeness of Jesus, which leads to a deeper knowledge of the Father and a greater likeness of the whole triune Godhead.

Unity and the Economic Trinity

The Economic Trinity as revealed throughout Scripture empha-sizes the diversity of the three members of the triune God in rela-tionship to creation, so in the previous section we focused on the diversity within the Trinity. The unity of the Trinitarian revelation must also be addressed. Several factors in Scripture help us see unity within the Trinity's economic activity.

Grounded in Monotheism

First, the entire unfolding of God's plan (*economia*) begins with God's self-revelation in the Old Testament. Here God emphatically declares to Israel that there is only one God and that Yahweh is that God (Deut. 6:14). Whereas in polytheism, pagans constantly struggle to balance their relationship with many gods, Israel knows that there is only one God, and all their attention is focused on him. This is reinforced by the first commandment that Israel shall have no other gods before Yahweh (Ex. 20:3); he alone is the One with whom they have to do.[15]

This focus on the one God undergirds the whole discussion of the Trinity. When we acknowledge the three persons within the Godhead, we are continually reminded that there is only one God who relates to his people. It is as though the triune God gave Israel time to comprehend that there is only one God, and then, with the New Testament, he begins to explain more fully what his oneness entailed. So the unfolding of the second and third persons of the Trinity in the New Testament must be understood in the context of Old Testament monotheism, and that monotheism must now be understood against the background of the Trinity.

In light of the New Testament revelation, we normally identify the work of Yahweh in the Old Testament primarily with that of God the Father. This is because when Jesus refers to Yahweh, he refers to him as his Father (e.g., John 20:17). Rarely does Jesus

---

15. Kaufmann, *The Religion of Israel*, Chapter 3.

refer just to God. A case could be made, however, that Yahweh in the Old Testament may well be a picture of an undifferentiated Trinity.[16] Nevertheless, the New Testament references to God that are not otherwise spelled out normally refer to God the Father (see 2 Cor. 13:14). So the New Testament church along with the early church tended to identify Yahweh of the Old Testament with God the Father. The effect of this is a further grounding of the unity of the Godhead in the monotheism of the Old Testament.

THE ROLES OF GOD

In the Old Testament Yahweh makes himself known in eight major roles (Creator, King, Personal Revealer, Priest, Judge, Father, Redeemer, and Shepherd) and a number of minor roles (Physician, Warrior, Teacher, Prophet, Friend, Husband, and Bridegroom). God makes himself known through these roles, which by analogy tell us the way God works in relationship to his creation. They are figures of speech borrowed from our world to draw comparisons with who God is and how we relate to him.[17]

The key thing is to notice that when Jesus and the Spirit appear in the New Testament, they do the same kinds of work that the Father does in the Old Testament. This means that they function in all of the same roles as Yahweh does. For example, while God as Creator gives life in the Old Testament, the New Testament speaks of the Son as giving life (John 1:4), while the Spirit is also described as having the same capacity (2 Cor. 3:6). The value of understanding these roles is that they provide part of the data that point to the divinity of both the Son and the Spirit.[18] The roles strengthen the unity of the Economic Trinity by indicating that the Father, Son,

---

16. See the references to the implicit plurality of God in the Old Testament in the discussion of the Messiah, the Spirit, the Wisdom and the Word of God in Chapter 2. See also Toon, *Our Triune God.*

17. Coppedge, *Portraits of God,* 26–33.

18. Coppedge, *Portraits of God,* 366–71.

and Spirit work in a similar way.[19] They do the same things in relationship to the world even when the emphasis is different. The oneness of God provides a natural explanation for how all members of the Trinity have a similar way of working.

THE EXTERNAL OPERATIONS OF THE TRINITY ARE INDIVISIBLE: *OPERA AD EXTRA SUNT INDIVISA*

Additionally, the unity of the Economic Trinity is boosted in the New Testament by the fact that all members of the Trinity share in the role that distinguishes each individual member. So the New Testament makes clear that while the Father is primarily responsible for creation, both Jesus (John 1:3; Col. 1:16; Heb. 1:1–3) and the Spirit (2 Cor. 3:3, 6) are involved in bringing creation into existence. In the same way, while the Son carries a special responsibility in redemption, the Father sends the Son into the world and the Spirit conceives him in the incarnation. Both witness to him at his baptism, and sometimes the resurrection is attributed to the Father (Acts 2:32–33) and at other times to the Spirit (Rom. 1:3). The redeeming work of God is clearly the work of all three, even though the Son is primarily the Redeemer. The unified work of the three persons can especially be seen in Hebrews 9:14 and Ephesians 2:18, where they all contribute to our redemption.

In like manner, both the Father and the Son share in the work of the Spirit in sanctification (Rom. 15:16). The Father sends the Spirit at Pentecost at the request and with the assistance of the Son (Acts 2:33). So the Spirit's work in the world is clearly understood in terms of a joint work with the Father and the Son (John 14).

So while each member of the Trinity is identified with a special work in the economy of God, all three persons are involved in

---

19. Within some of the language of each role there will be variations of how each member functions. So in the family language, the first person functions as Father and the second as Son. The Spirit does not have a family title in the same way but functions within the family context, e.g., agent of new birth. This variation within each role protects us from assuming Jesus acts exactly like the Father. Rather, he relates as Son to Father within this family role language.

each of these three major activities of God in the world: creation, redemption, and sanctification. This accounts for the classic Latin phrase *opera ad extra sunt indivisa*: "the external operations of the Trinity are undivided."

The unity in the work of the Economic Trinity is best captured by the early church's concept of mutual indwelling, or *perichoresis*. Reflecting the teaching of John 14:10–11, 20 and John 17:21, *perichoresis* points to the inner penetration of each member of the Trinity with the others, so that each shares the life and the activity of the other two. Of course, *perichoresis* is also closely tied to the concept of *homoousios* in which the members of the Trinity share the same essence. *Homoousios* is grounded in the monotheism of God. All three persons of the Trinity share the same being because there is one God, and out of this shared existence (*perichoresis*) each one is involved in the activities of the other in relationship to the created world. The early church leaders grasped the unity of the persons but did not blur the distinctions. Thus they said that everything which could be said of the Father could be said of the Son and Spirit, except that the Father is not the Son or Spirit. And the same is true for the Son and Spirit. They can be distinguished only by their persons and unique relationships to each other, but cannot be distinguished by their attributes, authority, roles, or external actions towards creation. The persons are one in being.

CHAPTER FOUR

The Triune God Within Himself

HOW THE ECONOMIC TRINITY REVEALS THE ONTOLOGICAL TRINITY

THE RELATION OF THE Trinity to creation comes clear to us through God's unfolding revelation of himself in Scripture. From the Scriptural data, we have every reason to believe that we are being told about one triune God not two.[1] This means that the question of how God relates *within himself* should certainly be consistent with what he has made known *about himself* in his relationship to the world. The central fact about their being is that all three persons share the same essence (*homoousios*).[2] We discover this in part from the data about how God reveals himself in the Economic Trinity. On the basis of Jesus' own teaching, we are given explicit warrant to move

---

1. An example of the contrary position is Gruenler in *The Trinity in the Gospel of John*, xvii. Gruenler argues that in the economy of redemption the Son and the Spirit have "modes of operation," reflected in their subordination to the Father, that are not the same as the way the Ontological Trinity works in "modes of being."

2. See T. F. Torrance, "The *homoousion* is the ontological/epistemological lynch pin of Christian theology" (*The Christian Doctrine of God*, 92–98).

from the Economic Trinity to the Ontological Trinity. This task begins with Scripture and draws out its theological implications.[3]

The clearest indication we have of the persons of the Trinity comes in our understanding of the Son as he is made known in the incarnation. Once the Son is fully revealed, we are in a position to discuss the Ontological Trinity. The Father begets the Son and breathes the Spirit, so the second and third persons of the Trinity have their ontological "origin" in the Father. In terms of our knowing God (our epistemology) we begin with Jesus and the Economic Trinity. However, with the being of God (our ontology), we focus our attention on the role of the Father and the Ontological Trinity.

The Economic Trinity helps us understand the Ontological Trinity; they are complementary. In the economic activity of God, the Father is described as the head of Christ (1 Cor. 11:3). This is seen when it is repeatedly stated that the Son is sent by the Father (e.g., John 20:21), demonstrating the Father's direction over the Son. Likewise, the Spirit is sent from the Father through the Son in such a way that he does not speak for himself but calls attention to what has been said by the Father through the Son (John 16:13–15). So when we think of the Trinity in economic terms, it seems that the Son sees himself under the direction of the Father, even though they are in intimate communion. In the same way, the Spirit, who does not speak on his own, is pictured as being under the direction of the Father and the Son. Again, in spite of intimate relationships (sometimes he is described as Spirit of the Father and sometimes as the Spirit of the Son), he does not act independently but under their direction.

---

3. For an alternative approach, see the work of David Coffey, who believes the biblical doctrine of the Trinity is not to be identified with the Economic Trinity. The biblical doctrine should lead us to an understanding of the Ontological/ Immanent Trinity and that understanding of the Trinity should then help us understand the Economic Trinity. The value of Coffey's work is to remind us there is a reciprocity of one view of the Trinity illuminating another (*Deus Trinitas*, 16ff).

If the being (ontology) and function (economy) of the Trinity are the same reality, then the functional descriptions suggest that there is a similar ordering in the being of the Trinity. While there is no subordination (i.e., that the Son or the Spirit is inferior or less fully divine than the Father), there is an order in social relationships, even within the Godhead. We are now in a position to more fully understand the internal work of the triune God.

THE ONTOLOGICAL TRINITY:
OPERA AD INTRA

The internal working of the Trinity (*opera ad intra*) centers on the very essence of God. For this reason, the discussion of the being of God (ontology) has customarily been described in terms of the Ontological Trinity. Some authors call this the "Immanent Trinity," a few writers prefer the "Social Trinity," still others talk about the "Relational Trinity." Each term has its strengths and weaknesses, but we will use the traditional "Ontological Trinity" to talk about the *opera ad intra*.

THE DISTINCTNESS OF PERSONS

The distinctness of the persons may be understood in terms of the personal identities of the members of the Trinity. The key way in which the persons of the Trinity are distinguished in their being is that the Father is the fountainhead of divinity (*fons totius divinitas*). Sometimes this is described in terms of the Father being the source of divinity, as long as "source" is not understood in a temporal sense. A son cannot exist without a father; the father is the source or origin of the son. So the distinction between Father and Son is that the Father begets the Son and the Son is begotten of the Father. The distinctness is that one begets and the other is begotten. The early church was careful to identify this relationship as an *eternal* begetting so there would be no confusion between divine relationships and the analogous human relationships, where a father begets a son in time. In this divine relationship, there was never a time when the Son did not exist.

If the Father is the fountainhead of divinity in terms of begetting the Son, his role in relationship to the Spirit is that the Spirit proceeds from the Father through the Son. Accordingly, the Spirit is described as breathed or aspirated. The classic distinction between the Son and the Spirit is that one is begotten and the other is breathed. The persons are distinguished in that they are non-interchangeable, neither confused nor fused, but have unique and permanent names and distinctive relationships.

The early church leaders were fully aware that they were working with analogies that did not fully explain all of the mystery of the Trinity. They were trying to be faithful to the biblical data. When they had gone that far, they realized they could not go much further. They were conscious that these analogies are imperfect and there is much that is wrapped in mystery. But the appeal to mystery should not obscure the real gains made. The result was that they had a concept of the Son being eternally begotten by the Father and the Spirit eternally breathed by him. "Begetting" and "breathing" are valuable terms because they convey both oneness and separateness, and both are tied to the central concept of life. They show intimate connection between triune persons while preserving distinctness. They are imperfect terms, but they are also valuable personal terms that helped the church move forward a major step in understanding the internal relations of the Trinity.[4]

EQUALITY AND ONENESS: UNITY OF THE TRINITY

ONE ESSENCE

The debate in the early church was first over the divinity of Christ and then over the divinity of the Spirit. This discussion led

---

4. Lossky, *The Mystical Theology of the Eastern Church*, 23–43.

to the holistic view that the biblical data presents the three persons as sharing the same essence or substance. The development of the term *homoousios* was the shorthand form to say that all three persons are of the same nature. They are not merely *like* each other (*homoiousios*) but they are of the *same essence* (*homoousios*). Thus the persons of the Trinity equally share in the divine being.

What is this one nature (*ousia*) shared by the persons of the Trinity? The most pervasive biblical answer to this question is that the essence of God is mostly aptly described as holiness. God reveals his holiness beginning at Sinai (Lev. 11:44–45) and continuing straight through Scripture to the end of the New Testament (1 Pet. 1:14–16). When visions of God's being are given in both Testaments, heavenly creatures declare his holiness (Isa. 6:3; Rev. 4:8). Further, the biblical titles for God and the persons of the Trinity are "the Holy One of Israel," "Holy Father," "the Holy One of God," and, of course, "the Holy Spirit." No other term is used so pervasively for God than his holiness. While other terms have been suggested (e.g., good, sovereign), in Scripture none carry the weight or the pervasiveness that holiness does in describing the essence of the divine nature. The basis for triune unity is in God's holy essence.

The church has historically take two approaches to describing the unity of this holy God. The Western church tends to ground God's unity in the substance of God. God first exists, and then he exists as Trinity, or as three persons. The ontological principle of God's unity is not found in the persons but in the one substance or being of God.

Alternatively, the Eastern church grounded the unity of God in the person of the Father. Here the Father is the "cause" of both the generation of the Son and the breathing of the Spirit. So the ontological principle of unity is traced back to a person. This results in a heightened focus on the persons of the Trinity. The three persons, who coinhere and share a relational life, are not simply used to explain God's diversity but also to provide the explanation for his unity. Of the two options, this seems more satisfactory.[5]

Recently T. F. Torrance has set forward a third means of describing the unity of God. He points out that some of the Eastern fathers—Athanasius, Gregory of Nazianzus, and Didymus the Blind—questioned the widespread Eastern notion of finding the unity of God in the Father. Their reservations were related to the fear that making the Father the "cause" of the others might lead to subordinationism. They suggested that God's unity was better found in his triunity, centered in his perichoresis. Here the monarchy of God is not limited to the Father. The Son and Spirit do not derive their being from the Father but have their being in triunity: Trinity in unity, unity in Trinity. So the persons derive only their personhood, their personal differences as Father, Son, and Spirit, from the other persons, but not their oneness and being. Their unity comes in a mutual perichoretic sharing of life and existence together.[6]

HOLINESS/LOVE AND PERSONS

Because the Bible describes God as holy in essence, then the three persons too must be understood as holy. This means holiness is not a "thing" but rather is personally based and therefore expressed in personal categories. In Scripture, holiness is described as personal in several ways, but the chief expression is love. Thus the holy God's steadfast love (*hesed*) is central to the Old Testament, and the triune God is described twice in the New Testament as love (1 John 4:7, 16).[7] Holiness expressed as love may be the best description of the *ousia* and therefore the unity of God.

Another factor in understanding the *ousia,* and therefore the *homoousios,* of the triune God is that this term is not defined primarily by Greek philosophy but by Hebrew thought. God, from the

---

5. Zizioulas, *Being as Communion*, 40–41 and 88–89.

6. See T. F. Torrance, *Trinitarian Perspectives* and *The Christian Doctrine of God.*

7. Zizioulas describes love as the supreme ontological predicate of God, that which constitutes his being (*Being as Communion*, 46).

Hebrew perspective, is not a static but a living and therefore personal being. God's revelation of himself to Moses at Mount Sinai—"I AM that I AM" (Ex. 3:14)—reveals that in essence he is personal. This idea gets clearer when we understand that the Son and the Spirit share this *ousia* of God—they are of the same substance (*homoousios*). So we have a personal and triune God sharing the essence of his being in holiness and love in an intrapersonal and conjunctive way.[8]

EQUALITY IN ATTRIBUTES OF DEITY

The unity of the Trinity is further seen in the fact that the three members share the attributes of the deity. These attributes may be grouped under four headings:

1. *Personal Attributes*—including the concepts of reason, imagination, emotions, and will that are expressed in life, sociality, freedom, morality, creativity, and responsibility.

2. *Moral Attributes*—require other persons for expression, and here the holiness of God is expressed first of all in self-giving love. Then holiness through love is seen in grace, goodness, truth, faithfulness, righteousness, and purity.

3. *Relative Attributes*—depend on the relationship of God to his creation for their expression. These include his omnipotence, omnipresence, omniscience, and wisdom.

4. *Absolute Attributes*—hold true apart from any relationship to the creation. They include the simplicity of God, his

---

8. T. F. Torrance, *The Christian Doctrine of God*, 116–25. Torrance puts it this way: "The being of God is to be understood as essentially personal, dynamic and relational being. The being of God is to be understood therefore, as living and dynamic being, fellowship-creating for communion-constituted being, but if it is communion-constituted being toward us it is surely to be understood also as an ever-living, ever-dynamic communion in the Godhead. By his very Nature he is a communion in himself." Torrance uses his brother's description as God's being is really "his Being-In-Communion" (J. B. Torrance, "Contemplating the Trinitarian Mystery of Christ," in *Alive to God*, 141).

infinity, including his eternity and immensity, his constancy, his aseity, and his perfection.[9]

The persons of the Trinity share in all four categories of attributes. The unity of the Godhead is found in that all three persons fully share in all classes of attributes and in each one of the attributes. This is the heart of the argument against ontological subordination within the triune God. The Father, Son, and Spirit are fully God, and by sharing fully the attributes of God no one is less divine or of less value than the others.

EACH EXISTS IN THE OTHERS

The unity of the Trinity is also established in terms of each person sharing the common essence and life of the others. The corollary to *homoousios* (same essence) is *perichoresis* (coinherence), which means that each member permeates and completely conditions the other two. The concept of *perichoresis* accents the mutuality of the persons of the Trinity in self-giving love to one another out of their holy nature.[10]

Perichoresis is often described in terms of light. This is one of the most pervasive analogies used by the early church in describing the Trinity. In fact, it is the only physical analogy that was used in the Nicene Creed, where the Son is described as "God from God, Light from Light." The church fathers also used the source of light, a ray of the light, and the illumination of light to depict the the members of the Trinity. Within the providence of God, a better understanding of the physical qualities of light has enhanced the analogy in our own day, describing the interpenetration of the life of the Trinity. A beam of light shining through a prism breaks it into different colored rays, like that of a rainbow. But a normal beam of light mixes the colors together. The single beam of light is analogous to the shared existence of the members of the Trinity united

---

9. A fuller discussion of all these attributes is provided in the next chapter.

10. For the theological role played by *perichoresis*, see T. F. Torrance, *The Christian Doctrine of God*, 102, 168–73.

in coinherence. The distinctive functions of the Economic Trinity are analogous to light shining through a prism. But these functional distinctions do not prevent each member of the Trinity from continuing to share through mutual permeation the common divine life of the others.

The concepts of *homoousios* and *perichoresis* together make it possible to understand the unity of the persons of the Trinity. The three perichoretically share the same essence (as in the holiness of God). This sharing of holy being is a personal and mutual self-giving between the persons of the Trinity and is expressed in holy love.[11]

DIVERSITY IN TRINITY: DIFFERENCE IN THREENESS

Having reviewed the distinctness of persons as well as their unity, we return now to examine how the persons of the Trinity relate to one another. If they are distinctly three but share a common essence, how do we conceive of the internal operations of the Trinity or the *opera ad intra*?[12]

In identifying the distinctness of the persons of the Trinity, we may say that the Father begets the Son and breathes the Spirit. The language is familial. Though the Father's breathing the Spirit is not as direct, the relations of Father and Son place family language at the center of our understanding of the Trinity.[13] Thus the relationships among the persons of the Trinity are best described in terms of self-giving love. If love is an expression of holiness, the *ousia* of God, then it is natural to see holiness in a shared life where there is also a mutual self-giving to one another in love. So the distinctness of the persons in terms of their personal identities assists in understanding how they relate in other-oriented love.[14]

---

11. For their own *perichoresis* as a movement/communion of love within the triune God, see T. F. Torrance, *The Christian Doctrine of God*, 171.

12. For discussion of the use of the language of "three persons," see Kasper, *The God of Jesus Christ*, 285–90.

13. It is very likely that the Spirit is not referred to in terms of mother so that the persons in the Trinity will be seen as transcending gender.

14. Richard of St. Victor, *The Twelve Patriarchs*, 9.

HOLY LOVE: A WESLEYAN SYSTEMATIC THEOLOGY

This is a new way of understanding all reality. It is based on person-to-person relationships growing out of holy, self-giving love. As Walter Kasper notes, "The ultimate reality . . . is the person who is fully conceivable only in the relationality of giving and receiving."[15] If this is an accurate understanding of the triune God, it sets the stage for an appropriate understanding of the way human persons should relate as well.

The distinctness between the persons is revealed by the Economic Trinity. The Father is the head, the Son is the one sent by the Father, and the Spirit proceeds from the Father through the Son. The content of Father's headship (1 Cor. 11) is defined by love (1 Cor. 13). Headship within the Trinity is not governed by God as King but by God as Father (of the Son). So the Father sends the Son and then the Spirit into the world as an expression of their threefold self-giving relationships to one another in love. The other-oriented love of the Ontological Trinity expresses itself in the sending of the Son and the Spirit in the Economic Trinity. So while there is a functional distinction within the economic activity of the Father sending the Son and the Spirit, this external act arises from an eternal, mutual self-giving within God. This onto-relational context of holiness in mutual self-giving love sets an entirely different context for understanding the functional roles of the Trinity. There is a possibility of both equality and mutual self-giving among persons while their external functioning with one another is ordered in a complementary way. All the external acts of God arise from one eternal nature and character of the Godhead. They all arise out of the holy love of Father for Son and Spirit.

This is the familial character of the Godhead. The Father, the head, begets the Son and breathes the Spirit, but he does so as a loving Father, not as sovereign King. The emphasis is not upon royal language but on family categories. The emphasis is not on kingship but paternity. The family relationships are not expressed

---

15. Kasper, *The God of Jesus Christ*, 310.

in terms of authority and submission but in terms of self-giving love, empowering grace, caring goodness, truthful communication, righteous relationships, and purity from self-centeredness. These characteristics express how the triune God relates internally within himself prior to expressing them to other persons.[16] They set the stage for an even clearer understanding of how the Trinity relates to persons in the created world, and subsequently how this then becomes a pattern for person-to-person relationships.

THE MYSTERY OF THE TRINITY

LIMITS OF OUR KNOWLEDGE

When we have correlated all of God's revelation in Scripture with our best understanding of how it fits together in our theology, we are fully aware that we still do not comprehend everything there is to know about God. We have enough knowledge to know that God is bigger than our understanding of him. If Scripture is true, we can understand all that we need to know to relate to God. So we have adequate knowledge, but we do not have comprehensive knowledge. We understand only in part.

The Eastern tradition of the church says we know God through his energies (activities/revelation), but in his essence God is unknowable. Known formally as *apophatic theology*, it suggests that we know the way God works, but in his inner being he cannot be fully known.[17]

This tradition reminds us that we do not have exhaustive knowledge about God. The case can be overstated, however, as though we

---

16. See Moltmann's description of the principle that relates the two understandings of the Trinity: "Statements about the Immanent Trinity must not contradict statements about the Economic Trinity. Statements about the Economic Trinity must correspond to doxological statements about the Immanent Trinity" (*The Trinity and the Kingdom*, 154, 158–61).

17. Lossky, *The Mystical Theology of the Eastern Church*, 23–43; Bobrinskoy, *The Mystery of the Trinity,* 303–16, 55–63.

know nothing about the essence of God.[18] The concept of revelation redresses the imbalance of a purely apophatic theology. What is clear from Scripture is that God has made himself known, and in the process he has revealed a great many things about himself. What we have is *true knowledge* but not *exhaustive knowledge*.[19] Athanasius captures the essence of the matter: "Thus far human knowledge goes. Here the cherubim spread the covering of their wings."[20]

Mystery helps us live with the limitations of our theology. Sometimes we gain knowledge from a trusted a authoritative source (revelation) without having a full explanation, which we usually desire. We sometimes have knowledge of *what* exists without being able to explain fully *why* or *how* it exists. And in Christian theology, we clearly understand that God *is* triune without fully knowing *how* he is so. The concept of mystery assists us with the willingness to live with partial but true knowledge. It means we do not need to know everything (exhaustive knowledge) before we can accept some things as true knowledge. Having said this, we do want to take advantage of all we can know. So, the next question is, Are there any parallels that may assist us for living with this mystery?

ANALOGIES OF TRINITY

Throughout the history of the church several helpful illustrations of the Trinity have emerged. Some of these illustrate the mystery of how three persons make up one Godhead. They have largely consisted of analogies. An analogy compares two things that are alike in some ways but not in every way. No analogy is perfect, and some are more limited than others. But analogies help us learn and give us some tools to conceptualize things we do not fully comprehend.

Analogies are not proofs of the doctrine of the Trinity. They are illustrations from our world that point to the Trinity in the

---

18. On the Eastern church and the unknowability of the Ontological Trinity through the *via negativa*, see La Cugna, *God for Us*, 44, 181–98.

19. For a valuable discussion of the concept of mystery in the tradition of the church, see Kasper, *The God of Jesus Christ*, 267–71.

20. Cited in T. F. Torrance, *The Christian Doctrine of God*, 81.

supranatural world.[21] Several analogies, verbal and pictorial, have been helpful.

PICTORIAL ANALOGIES

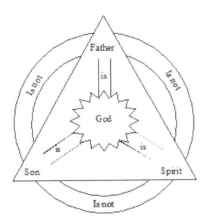

Figure 1. The Unity of God; The Distinctness of the Persons.

The purpose of Figure 1 is to indicate that the Father is God, the Son is God, and the Spirit is God, but the Father is not the Spirit, the Spirit is not the Son, and the Son is not the Father. The diagram indicates the unity of God and the distinctness of the persons. The equilateral triangle that forms the heart of the diagram has become a frequent symbol of the Trinity by indicating the equality, distinctness, and unity of the three persons in the Godhead.

The middle of the three ellipses suggests the inner, connected life of the three persons. This is the perichoretic existence of the Trinity. The outside of the ellipses suggests the distinctness of the persons.

ANALOGIES FROM CREATION

One of the analogies used in the early church was that of water, frequently described in a threefold manner: its source, its flow, and its collection together. Though there are variations on this, it might

---

21. Kasper, *The God of Jesus Christ*, 268.

HOLY LOVE: A WESLEYAN SYSTEMATIC THEOLOGY

well be described as a spring, a stream, and a lake. The key is that the same substance takes three different forms.

In our discussion of perichoresis we saw that light has been regularly used as a symbol of the Trinity. The early church often used the analogy of the source of light, a ray of light and its illumination of something. But a contemporary understanding of light might be more helpful. A single beam has multiple rays that create different colors, and running a beam of light through a prism separates the colors. The unified rays in a beam of light serve as an illustration of the inner penetration or *perichoresis* of the members of the Trinity.

A variation on this in the early church was the concept of one torch that lights two other torches by the same fire. So, it may sometimes be seen as three separate torches, but sometimes they are held together in one hand to form a common fire.

One advantage of this analogy is the connection of light in the Old and New Testaments as a symbol of the presence of God. This is related to the concept of God's holiness as brilliance, which was expressed when the glory of God descended on the mountain, the tabernacle, and the temple in the Old Testament (Ex. 19, 40; 1 Kgs. 8). This is seen even more clearly in the New Testament when Jesus says, "I am the light of the world" (John 8:12, 9:4). This biblical figure may be one of the most effective analogies we have from the physical world.

ANALOGIES FROM MUSIC

Spatial, verbal, and visual analogies have distinct limits. An auditory analogy may help us break out of some of those limitations. The experience of music seems particularly promising. Three notes sounded individually carry their own distinctness but when played together in a chord are experienced as one sound with three distinct components. A variation of this is three instruments playing the same note but with three distinct sounds that blend together in harmony. An extension of the same analogy would be three melodies intricately woven together in a polyphony of blended sounds within a symphony. The interactivity and multiplicity of the latter has a special attractiveness that draws a person into the experience of these audible sounds.[22]

The disadvantage of these analogies is that they leave out the personal dimension of God, and this is a serious limitation. Some have developed personal analogies, which we will examine next.

PERSONAL ANALOGIES

Augustine attempted to understand the Trinity in terms of a human individual made in the image of God. Much of Western theology followed Augustine on this point, looking for God's image within the human psyche rather than in relationships between persons. He suggested the internal, intrapersonal analogy of memory, understanding, and will, or alternatively, mind, knowledge, and love. While this was a positive attempt to connect the Trinity with people, who bear God's image, by looking to the psyche of one person he ruled out interpersonal relationships, which are fundamental to the Trinitarian data of Scripture. Augustine's analogies tend to make God more of a single unitary being rather than three persons in relationship.

Augustine offered an alternative that relates persons to one another. It is his description of the Trinity as the lover, the beloved, and the love between them. The Father is the lover, the Son the beloved, and the Holy Spirit is the love relationship between them. At least in regard to the lover and the loved, this analogy lends itself to interpersonal relations; unfortunately, making the Holy Spirit the love connection between the other two seems to depersonalize him. Thus the trifold relationship of the Trinity is not developed.

Better still is the interpersonal analogy suggested by Richard of Saint Victor (see Figure 2). He begins with a discussion of reciprocal love between two persons. But he broadens this to suggest that a

---

22. Begbie, "Through Music: Sound Mix," 150.

HOLY LOVE: A WESLEYAN SYSTEMATIC THEOLOGY

third dimension of real love comes when two people who love each other in turn love a third. It is in the shared love toward a third that love is fully expressed and enjoyed.

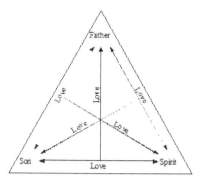

Figure 2. Three-dimensional Love by Richard of St. Victor.

The family would obviously seem to be an analogy closely tied to that of Richard (see Figure 3). Here we find a husband and wife mutually loving each other in unconditional, self-giving love. But when a child is born, they both share love for the child and expand their love for each other. Then the child and husband share love for the wife and the wife and child share love for the husband. So there is a multifaceted dimension of shared love expressive of shared love between Father, Son, and Spirit.

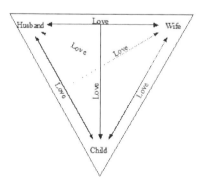

Figure 3. Family Love.

Some have shied away from the family analogy because of a desire to avoid any sexual overtones when discussing the nature of God. All analogies have limits. Nevertheless, the family (without gender or sexual overtones) may well be the best analogy of the interpersonal workings of God. This would certainly fit with Genesis 1 and 2 where God made man and woman in his image, which includes the interpersonal relationships of the family. Sin disrupts this pattern even before the family expands to include children, but the inference may still be drawn that God's intent is for people, who reflect his own social image, to have loving relationships with others. Unity *and* diversity, then, are the common experience of most family relationships, and this may help us conceive of the triune God.

CHAPTER FIVE

The Nature of the Triune God

THE TRADITIONAL APPROACH TO understanding God begins with the existence and attributes of God and then moves to a discussion of the triune nature of God. This has been particularly true in the West following the structure of Thomas Aquinas's *Summa Theologica*.[1] We are reversing this order, beginning with the triune God and then moving to God's attributes in light of his Trinitarian nature. Unlike Aquinas, we will not attempt to prove the existence of God with philosophical arguments, but like Scripture we assume the existence of God. The question for Israel and the early church was not, "Does God exist?" but "What is God like?" Because the full revelation of God discloses what he is like—triune—we are now ready to understand his nature and attributes.[2]

One thing that is obvious about the triune God is his personal nature. Because he is three persons in one being, his personhood is clearly primary and deserves priority attention. We will discuss the

---

1. Catherine La Cugna describes this discussion of the attributes of God without reference to the Trinity as a fruit of Thomas' theology that has led to the "marginalization of the doctrine of the Trinity" in *God for Us*, 150–67; see also Pannenberg, *Systematic Theology*, 280–83.

2. Pope treats the Trinity before he addresses the attributes of God in *A Compendium of Christian Theology*, 1:255–358. See also the contemporary approach of Robert Jenson, who begins with an elaborate discussion of the doctrine of the Trinity and then refuses to identify a separate section on "attributes" (*Systematic Theology*, 1:223).

personal being of the triune God through the personal attributes of God, attributes that provide us with the content of the concept of personhood.

Along with personhood two other characteristics of God control the biblical understanding of what he is like: his holiness and his love. Throughout the history of the church, love has been central to understanding the holy Trinity. This is not surprising in light of God's self-description, "I am holy" (Lev. 11:44–45; 1 Pet. 1:15–16) and the apostolic description, "God is love" (1 John 4:8, 16). Because both of these relate to God's essence, they should control our understanding of who he is as well as how we conceive his other attributes.

Here's the problem we face: on the one hand, we have God's essence, his holiness and love, and on the other his relationality. How do we put these components together? Is it possible to understand God's holiness in love as relational categories, how he relates within himself even before he relates to the world? Love is obviously a relational category, so it is not difficult to see how this may tie the essence and relationality of God together. But holiness is also relational; it describes how God relates within himself as well as to the created order. In some circles holiness and love have been understood only as moral attributes of God, but in reality, they are much more than that. They do relate to his moral nature and the way he relates to other persons, but in a transcendent sense, they are much more constitutive of his basic nature, out of which he relates.

HOLINESS OF THE TRIUNE GOD: THE FIRST INDICATOR OF THE BEING (*OUSIA*) OF GOD

Our understanding of God's holiness begins at Mount Sinai, where God tells Israel that he is looking for a holy people (Ex. 19:6) because he wants them to be like himself: "Be holy, for I am holy" (Lev. 11:44–45; see 19:2; 20:7, 8, 26; 21:8). In this same context the phrases, "I am the LORD" and "I am holy," are used interchangeably.

The parallelism is so striking that it is difficult not to see the two as synonymous throughout the book (Lev. 19:2–4, 10, 12, 14, 16, 18, 25, 28, 30–31, 34, 36, 37; 20:7, 8, 24, 26; 21:8, 15, 23; 22:2–3, 8–9, 16, 30–33). The recurrence of these two expressions all through the Sinai story strongly indicates that the chief idea being revealed about God is his holiness.

At significant points in Israel's history, further glimpses into the essential character of God are given, like the vision of Isaiah when he sees the creatures around the throne of God crying, "Holy, holy, holy is the LORD Almighty, the whole earth is full of his glory" (Isa. 6:3). This holy God enters into relationships with persons whom he wants to be holy, like himself. So the relational context where God makes his personal holy presence known dictates that our understanding of holiness be addressed in relational categories.

By the time we get to the New Testament, we find that all three persons of the Trinity are separately linked to the concept of holiness. The holiness of the Father is at key places in the New Testament story. In the Lucan birth narrative, Mary exclaims," Holy is his name" (Luke 1:49). At the beginning of his ministry, Jesus instructs his disciples to pray to the Father, "Hallowed be your name" (Matt. 6:9), and just before his crucifixion he prays to the "Holy Father" (John 17:11). Thus the holiness of the Father receives special mention at the incarnation as well as at the beginning and end of Jesus' ministry.

The New Testament writers reinforce God's holiness. Peter instructs the early Christians to be holy in all their conduct "for it is written, be holy, because I am holy" (1 Pet. 1:15, 16). The book of Revelation repeats the vision of Isaiah, where the creatures cry day and night, "Holy, holy, holy is the Lord God Almighty, who was and is and is to come!" (Rev. 4:8). It is as though the author is saying that God *has been* holy, *is* holy, and *will be* holy.

The New Testament also refers to the second and third persons of the Trinity as holy. In the angel's announcement to Mary, he says,

"The holy one to be born will be called the Son of God" (Luke 1:35). Further, at the outset of Jesus' ministry he is recognized as "the Holy One of God " (Mark 1:24; John 6:69; see also Acts 3:14). The leaders of the early church also regularly identify Jesus with the "Holy One" from Psalm 16:10 (Acts 2:27; 13:35) and refer to him as God's holy servant (Acts 3:13–14; 4:26, 30).[3]

The Spirit of God is called the "Holy Spirit" three times in the Old Testament (Ps. 51:11; Isa. 63:10–11) and no fewer than ninety-one times in the New Testament. This is by far the most common expression for God's Spirit. Holiness represents the essential nature of the triune God: Father, Son, and Spirit. It is the only qualifying adjective so attached to the names of the three.[4] Gustaf Aulén in his *Faith of the Christian Church,* expresses his conviction that "holiness is the foundation on which the whole conception of God rests."[5]

The fact that the holiness of God is attributed to the Father, the Son, and the Spirit is a further indicator of the important of this term. That all three persons are holy is suggestive of their essential unity, and at the same time that the term is relational. Each of the three are holy in their relationship to each other, so P. T. Forsyth can write, "Everything in Christian theology begins and ends with the holiness of God."[6]

What are the implications of God's holiness for a theological understanding of his nature? The extensiveness of the biblical data means that holiness is the first component of the essence, the *ousia,* of God's being. Because all three persons of the Trinity share the same being they all share in his holiness. This is a central

---

3. The "Holy One" is used of Jesus in Mark 1:24; Luke 4:34; John 6:69; Acts 2:27; 3:14; 13:15; 1 John 2:20; Rev. 3:7; see also Luke 1:35; Heb. 7:26.

4. Brunner, *The Christian Doctrine of God,* 157. See Procksch, "ἅγιος," *TDNT* 1:101; Muilenburg, "Holiness," *IDB* 2:623; Wood, "Holiness," *ZPEB* 3:180.

5. Aulén, *The Faith of the Christian Church,* 103. See also Vriezen, *An Outline of Old Testament Theology,* 151; *ISBE,* 2:725; *TDNT,* 1:114, 110; see also 93, 100. Rudolf Kittel asserts that the idea of holiness is not just one side of God's essential being but "rather is the comprehensive designation for the total content of the divine being in his relationship to the external world" (*NSRE,* 5:317).

6. Forsyth, *The Cruciality of the Cross,* 23–24.

aspect of the biblical data behind the *homoousios* of the members of the Trinity.

LOVE AND THE HOLY, TRIUNE GOD: THE SECOND INDICATOR OF THE BEING (*OUSIA*) OF GOD

HOLINESS AND LOVE

The relationship between God's love and God's holiness does not begin with the New Testament.[7] It is also part of God's self-revelation in the Old Testament and is closely tied to two key Hebrew words for love: *hesed* and *āhēb*.

HESED

God's love is related to his holiness in the first passage in Scripture that speaks about the holiness of God. "Who is like you—majestic in holiness . . . . In your *unfailing love* you will lead the people you have redeemed (Ex. 15:11, 13, emphasis added). The word translated "unfailing love" in the NIV is the Hebrew word *hesed*. It is a covenant term and therefore a relational term whose meaning is one of the richest in Scripture. It refers to God's love but also includes his grace, mercy, faithfulness and goodness, and therefore is translated variously as "steadfast love," "faithful love," "loving kindness," and "mercy." Thus it does not exclusively relate to love but has love at its center, and therefore it is one of the terms that appropriately describes a loving God.[8]

After God calls Israel to be a holy people (Ex. 19:6) and spells out for them what this holiness will mean in their lives (Ex. 20:1–17),

---

7. On the biblical data relating holiness and love, see Coppedge, *Portraits*, 244–52.

8. On the concept of *hesed,* see Snaith, *Distinctive Ideas of the Old Testament*, 94–130; Toon, "Lovingkindness," *EDT,* 661–62; Glueck, Hesed *in the Bible*; Sakenfeld, *The Meaning of* Hesed *in the Hebrew Bible*; Harris, "*hesed,*" *TWOT*, 1:305–7; Procksch, "ἅγιος," *TDNT*, 1:96–101.

he says he will manifest his steadfast love to thousands of those who are responding properly to this standard of holiness (Ex. 20:6; Deut. 5:20; Ps. 33:21, 22). In Isaiah "the Holy One of Israel" declares, "My unfailing love for you will not be shaken" (Isa 54:10, 7–8).[9]

The *hesed* of the Lord, which focuses upon his steadfast love but also includes elements of grace, mercy, and faithfulness, is best understood as a major expression of the holiness of God. The picture is of a holy God relating in covenant love to his people, revealing the relational nature of both holiness and love.[10]

AHEB

The second Hebrew word that describes the love of God is the more common word for love, 'ahēb. This word is first used in Deuteronomy, when God has Moses review Israel's history. In this theological review 'ahēb is used to describe God's love for Israel (Deut. 4:37). God tells Israel that they "are a people holy to the LORD your God" (Deut. 7:6; 14:2, 21; 26:19; also 28:9). The Lord did not choose Israel "because you were more numerous than other peoples, for you were the fewest of all peoples. But it was because the LORD loved you . . ." (Deut. 7:7–8).

God's love is a clear expression of his holy character as he seeks a holy people. Therefore, love becomes a manifestation of God's holiness, particularly at the point of the election of Israel. This passage not only relates holiness and love but also parallels God's love ('ahēb), and God's steadfast love (*hesed*).[11] Other passages also indi-

---

9. Wood, "Holiness," *ZPEB*, 3:183. On love as an expression of holiness, see Beckwith, "Holiness," *NSRE*, 5:318; Muilenburg, "Holiness," *IDB*, 2:622; Moody, *The Word of Truth*, 104; Procksch, "ἅγιος," *TDNT*, 1:93; McComisky, "qadosh," *TWOT*, 2:788.

10. See the combination of *hesed* and fatherhood in Isa. 63:7–8,10, 16; Jer. 31:9, 3. For the relation between God's steadfast love and his role as Husband, see Isa. 54:5–10 and Hos. 2:19.

11. For other Old Testament references to God's love, see Deut. 23:5; 1 Kgs. 10:9; 2 Chron. 2:11; 9:8; 2 Sam. 12:24; Ps. 47:4; 146:8; Prov. 3:12; 12:9; Isa. 43:4; 48:14; 63:9; Jer. 31:3; Mal. 1:2; Hos. 3:1; 11:4; 14:4; and Zeph. 3:17.

cate that love was the key motivation for a holy God electing his people (Isa. 43:4; 63:9; Jer. 31:3; Mal. 1:2; Hos. 11:1, 9).[12]

AGAPE

A third biblical word that describes the love of God is the Greek term *agapē*. This is a unique word adopted by the New Testament writers to express the unconditional, self-giving love of God. It is distinct from *eros,* which relates a romantic and physical love, which must possess its object. It differs further from *phileō,* which better describes friendship, companionship, and family love. *Agapē* is a supranatural love that has the special good and concern of the love object as its focus. It has an unconditionality and an other-centeredness about it that is distinct from the other words used for love in Greek. It is particularly used in the New Testament to describe the love of God the Father, Son, and Holy Spirit, and the kind of love God implants in the hearts of those who become his spiritual children.[13]

The picture of *agapē* as an expression of God's holy character is seen most clearly in John 17. Here Jesus addresses God as "holy Father." The intimacy of the love relationship between the Father and the Son is seen when Jesus talks about how the Father has loved him (John 17:23–24, 26).

The centrality of Jesus for tying together the holiness and the love of God becomes clearer when Jesus, the "Holy One of God" (John 6:69), reveals the love generated from the Economic Trinity. Jesus makes known the full love of the Father and the Spirit through

---

12. On love ('āhēb) see Snaith, *Distinctive Ideas,* 131–42; Alden, "אהב," *TWOT,* 1:14–15; Quell, "αγάπη," *TDNT,* 1:21–25; Stählin, "φιλέω," *TDNT,* 9:124–27, 154–60; Wallis, "אהב," *TDOT,* 1:99–117; McCarthy, "Notes on the Love of God in Deuteronomy," *CBQ,* 27, 144–47; Kay, "Man's Love for God in Deuteronomy," *VT,* 22:426–35.

13. On *agapē* see Quell, Stauffer, "αγάπη," *TDNT,* 1:21–55; Günther and Link, "Love," *NIDNTT,* 2:542–547; Harrelson, "The Idea of Agape in the New Testament, *JR,* 31:169–82; Morris, *The Testaments of Love*; Nygren, *Agape and Eros*; Outka, *Agape: An Ethical Analysis*; Spicq, *Agape in New Testament*; and Warfield, "The Terminology of Love," *PTR,* 16:1–45.

his own life in this world (John 13:1, 34–35; 14:21; 15:13–14; 16:27). All of this is part of the data indicating that the love of God is the second indicator of the being (*ousia*) of God and that this essence is relational in nature.

A Holy and Loving Triune God (Order of Being)

There is good biblical evidence that holiness originally expressed itself in at least six different ways, and one of those has several sub-meanings.[14] The six meanings include holiness as separation, power, brilliance, righteousness, goodness, and love. Brilliance may be subdivided in such a way that the immanent presence of God is made known in truth/faithfulness but also in terms of grace and purity.[15]

In the Old Testament, holiness expressed in righteous relationships leads to purity. When holiness is expressed as love, it manifests itself in both the grace of God and his goodness toward others. And when holiness is understood as truth, it is closely connected with God's faithfulness. While these moral attributes of God are scattered throughout the Old Testament, they are best understood in light of the unifying and integrating holiness of God.

In the New Testament, the multiple expressions of holiness are centered on the person of Jesus. He is the model for what a holy God looks like. Above all he is the central expression of the holy triune God in self-giving love. While Jesus is the Holy One of God (John 6:69), the earthly manifestation of the Economic Trinity, he also reveals holiness and love as the essence of the Ontological Trinity. Jesus' emphasis on love in relationship to holiness makes these the controlling concepts for understanding all the other moral attributes of God.

Understanding Jesus as the center of the Economic Trinity requires a theological move in understanding the essence (*ousia*)

---

14. Coppedge, *Portraits*, 51–52.
15. Coppedge, *Portraits*, 134–39, 174–76.

of the Ontological Trinity. A growing understanding of love signifi-cantly expands the concept of holiness as the essence of who God is. Love does not displace holiness as the *ousia* of God but amplifies it (John 17:11, 17, 23, 26). Thus, the holiness of God expressed in love in the Old Testament now finds such an expansion of love in the New Testament that it may be properly understood along with holiness as part of the *ousia,* or essence, of God.

There are two significant implications of this movement. First, the expanded understanding of the essential character of love fur-ther accents the relational character of the holiness of the triune God. If love in fact is the dominant expression of holiness, then holiness must be understood as a part of the essential relational-ity of God as a social being. Second, while holiness is expressed through the moral attributes of God in several ways, the concept of love now conjoined with holiness begins to determine the character of these other moral attributes. This means that holiness and love should control our understanding of other such moral characteris-tics as righteousness and purity, truth and faithfulness, grace and goodness.[16]

Having now examined the two foundational elements of God's being, we are now ready to evaluate the other attributes of this holy and loving triune God.

---

16. On the relationship between holiness and love, see Oden, *The Living God,* 123–25.

CHAPTER SIX

The Personal and Moral Attributes of the Triune God

THE ATTRIBUTES OF THE HOLY AND LOVING TRIUNE GOD

WHEN WE SPEAK ABOUT the characteristics of God, we use the term *attributes*.[1] One of the ways to understand the nature of the triune God is to understand God's attributes in light of his Trinitarian nature. Focusing on the three-personned God entails a significant shift in understanding how the attributes of God relate to each other. The Trinitarian approach, for example, affects the traditional order in which the attributes of God are described, with those coming first having some natural implications for those that are described later. The result is that the traditional classification of attributes gives way to a Trinitarian reordering of the attributes in light of the essential nature of God.

---

1. Other terms that have been used are *appellations, virtues, proprieties,* and *perfections.*

THE TRADITIONAL CLASSIFICATION OF ATTRIBUTES

Traditionally, classifying God's attributes has taken this form:

1. Absolute attributes: aseity, spirituality, infinity, and immutability
2. Relative attributes: omnipotence, omniscience, omnipresence, and wisdom
3. Personal attributes: personhood (social being, life, reason, imagination, emotions, and will)
4. Moral attributes: holiness, love, righteousness, purity, truth/faithfulness, grace, and goodness

This approach begins with the absolute attributes, that is, what God is in himself apart from his creation. Next come the relative attributes, which describe how this God relates to the created world, and then the personal attributes, and finally, the moral attributes, which express how God chooses to relate to other persons.[2]

THE TRINITARIAN APPROACH TO ATTRIBUTES

While the traditional classification of attributes is the standard for writing systematic theology, a case can be made for beginning with a Trinitarian approach, which would order the attributes like this:

1. Personal attributes
2. Moral attributes
3. Relative attributes
4. Absolute attributes

The rationale for this approach is that it more closely follows Scripture, which spends far more time revealing God's personal and moral attributes than his relative and absolute attributes. In fact, God's relative and absolute attributes are largely inferences drawn from what Scripture explicitly says about God's personal and moral

---

2. For the variety of classifications and language concerning the sequence of the attributes, see Oden, *The Living God*, 50–52.

attributes. The clear and explicit references should take precedence over the less direct inferences. But even more important, if God is a personal, Trinitarian being, then his personal and moral attributes should be the primary way to understand God, not only in the order of knowing but also in the order of being.

The advantages of this Trinitarian approach are significant. First, it gives the biblical data priority over the more philosophically oriented categories that emphasize the absolute and relative attributes of God. This is particularly significant because the absolute and relative categories tend to be more influenced by Greek philosophy than by biblical revelation. Second, a basic interpretive principle is followed in which the clear and biblically primary (personal and moral attributes) interprets the less clear (relative and absolute attributes). Third, the Trinitarian approach keeps the personal nature of the Trinity central, from an economic as well as an ontological perspective. Fourth, this approach allows us to address some of the problems of Classical Theism in articulating the relative and absolute attributes.

This will become clearer in interpreting certain attributes such as the omnipotence or the immutability of God. Approaching these from the personal and moral character of God rather than in terms of the absolute and relative attributes of a sovereign monarch casts an entirely different light upon them.

THE PERSONAL ATTRIBUTES
OF THE TRIUNE GOD

Trinitarian Theism expands our understanding of the personal attributes of God. This begins by focusing on the three persons of God rather than on an abstract understanding of the unity of God. This classic approach of the Eastern church is being revived in the

Western church by the recent interest in the Trinity.[3] Because the personal attributes of God relate not only to God but also to human persons, it is important to pay attention to them.

THE CENTRALITY OF JESUS

In discussing the personal character of God we are immediately confronted with the meaning of "person." What are the defining characteristics of a person, or what constitutes personhood? Jesus is the key to understanding what it means to be a person.

Beginning with our principles, first, that the Economic Trinity makes known the Ontological Trinity, and, second, that the Son is the key to understanding the Economic Trinity, we know the Father and the Spirit through Jesus (John 1:18). This is possible because they share the substance of God (*homoousios*). As Jesus puts it, "Anyone who has seen me has seen the Father" (John 14:7). As a result, to fully understand the personal nature of God, we look at the person of Jesus as he is revealed in the New Testament. One divine person, Jesus, makes known the other divine persons, the Father and Spirit, within the triune Godhead.

A corollary concept also illuminates personhood. Jesus is not only a divine person but also a human person. Not only is Jesus consubstantial (*homoousios*) with the Father and the Spirit, he is also consubstantial with human beings. He is the God-Man who reveals not only what God is like but also what God intends us to be. Jesus is the key to understanding theology *and* anthropology.[4]

So while Jesus is the full revelation of personhood, divine and human, he is also the full revelation of the image of God, which men and women bear. This means that personhood is closely identified in humans with the image of God. God made men and women in his own image so that they would be a reflection on earth of what he—the personal God—is like. Sin has distorted this image, so we do

---

3. See Grenz, *Rediscovering the Triune God*, 218–19.
4. On the development of the theological concept of person, see T. F. Torrance, *The Christian Doctrine of God*, 156–61.

not see clearly from sinful humanity what personhood ought to look like. But Jesus came in the full image of God *and* the full image of humanity. Therefore, he reveals in himself divine personhood and human personhood.

This full connection of the divine with the human in Jesus is called the *hypostatic union* This makes it possible to understand what it means to be a person. In this hypostatic union, the divine and human Jesus reveals what a person is in the divine sense and in the human sense. According to God's original intention, one is the mirror image of the other. Human persons are designed to be like divine persons. That is, humanity is to be in the image of God. In this chapter we will identify the components of personhood as they relate to the triune God. This will give us helpful categories for understanding persons when we consider topics in anthropology.[5]

THE COMPONENTS OF PERSONHOOD

Persons are obviously complex beings. But this complexity comprises a whole that we recognize as persons. Understanding the component parts of personhood will help us understand the whole, which in turn will help us better understand the several parts and how they fit together. In addition, this discussion will also help us identify the personal attributes of God.

SOCIAL NATURE

The first thing Jesus makes clear is that there are no persons in isolation. Personhood always includes an intricate web of relationships. This means that social communion and fellowship are right at the heart of the concept of personhood.[6] In other words, a person

---

5. For discussion of the origin of the concept of personhood, see Zizioulas, *Being as Communion*, 27–65.

6. Referring to God as a social being does not mean endorsing all the current theories of the social Trinity. Some, following the lead of Moltmann, have so closely identified the relational nature of God with social human communities that the the Trinity devolves into tritheism. By "social being," we are referring to God's relational nature within himself. The emphasis is on the perichoretic interrelatedness of the three divine persons.

is someone who is in vital relationship with others. Therefore a person is not complete in himself, that is, completeness is found in social relationships with other persons. An isolated person is to be incomplete. Thus a person is always a "being in communion."[7] This of course help explain the unity and diversity within the triune God. If persons are incomplete in themselves, the Father, So, and Spirit are only fully personal when they are joined together with other persons, which points to the unity of complete personhood within the triune God.[8]

We see the social nature of a person in both Jesus' human and divine relationships. From his birth Jesus related to his mother and father, and later to brothers and sisters. As he began his ministry, Jesus drew disciples around him. So he was always in relationships with other persons; he was not isolated. We cannot understand him apart from this network of relationships.

From the divine side, the birth narratives make it clear that the Father sent his Son into the world and that the Son was conceived by the Holy Spirit. The three divine persons were involved in the coming of Jesus. At his baptism the heavenly Father blesses his Son with whom he is pleased, and the Spirit of God anoints him for ministry. Jesus did the work of God within the parameters of these relationships. Clearly, he lived under the direction of the Spirit, and he constantly referred to his relationship with his Father.

At the end of his ministry, on his last night with the disciples, Jesus refers to God as his Father more than fifty times, and he prepares his disciples for the coming of the Spirit in their lives. In Acts 1–2 Jesus returns to the Father and then pours out the Spirit on his disciples. All of this indicates the close, intimate relationship between Jesus, the Father, and the Spirit.

---

7. For a discussion of how Athanasius and the Cappadocians helped transform the concept of substance to give it a relational character, see Zizioulas, *Being as Communion*, 83–89.

8. See Jenson's discussion of the community of personhood in *Systematic Theology,* 1:117–23.

When Jesus unfolds his own divine identity, he does it in terms of relatedness.[9] By describing himself as the Son of God who relates to God as Father, Jesus makes it clear that he is not self-originating. Thus the early church said he is eternally begotten of the Father. Nor is Jesus self-sustaining. His life is drawn continuously from the Father. Nor is he self-explanatory. By definition, a son finds his identity in relationship to his father. Nor is he self-fulfilling. He did not come to do his own will but the will of his Father. His fulfillment is in doing his Father's will, not his own.

Jesus expresses the social nature of personhood in terms of reciprocal relationships of love. Jesus' relationship to the Father and the Spirit are by their very nature reciprocal. There is full interaction between them. God accomplishes revelation and redemption from the Father through the Son in the Spirit (Eph. 2:18). Though they are uniquely distinct, they are not independent. They are always in relationship with one another, and they exist in mutual giving and receiving.[10]

T. F. Torrance uses the term "onto-relational" to describe the relationship of God's social character to his essence:

> No divine person is who he is without essential relation to the other two, and yet each divine person is other than and distinct from the other two. They are intrinsically interrelated not only through the fact that they have one Being in common so that each of them is in himself the whole God, but also in virtue of their differentiating characteristics as Father, Son, or Holy Spirit which hypostatically intertwine with one another and belong constitutively to their indivisible unity within the Trinity. There is an indivisible and continuous relation of being between the Father, the Son, and the Holy Spirit so that the being of the Godhead is

---

9. For further discussion of personhood that connects individuals and relationships, see Coffey, *Deus Trinitas*, 66–76.

10. For persons in a relationship centered in love, see Moltmann, *The Trinity in the Kingdom*, 171–74.

HOLY LOVE: A WESLEYAN SYSTEMATIC THEOLOGY

understood to be whole or complete not in the Father only but in the Son and in the Holy Spirit as well.[11]

Two further components of personhood seem to be particularly significant. One is life; the other is the functional capacities of personhood.[12]

LIFE

To be a person is to have life. Jesus makes clear that he possesses life in himself (John 1:4), and life is given to him from the Father and he shares this life with others (John 5:21). "For as the Father has life in himself, so he has granted the Son also to have life in himself" (John 5:26; 14:6). Within the triune Godhead this life is shared in a perichoretic way, and this perichoretic life is an essential component of personhood. Jesus brings the life of the triune God to human persons, and he models this life not only in its divine dimension but also in its human manifestation (John 10:10).

All persons have the capacity to perceive reality in which they exist. All persons are self-consciousness; that is, they have the ability to distinguish their own selves from the rest of reality. Through this self-consciousness all persons understand their own identities. Each individual person is unique, and each recognizes that he is distinct from other persons and all other reality.

The same is true of Jesus. He not only is able to perceive reality—he is conscious of the world—he is self-conscious. His chief way of describing himself in relationship to God is as a Son to the Father (Luke 2:49). Thus he distinguishes himself from the Father and from the Spirit (John 14:16–17). So he is not identical with either the Father or the Spirit; he has his own identity as the Son. At the same time, he does not see himself as separable from the Father or

---

11. T. F. Torrance, *The Christian Doctrine of God*, 157. See Torrance's excellent discussion on the giving and receiving of love within the triune God as a basis for God's expression of love toward us (162–67).

12. See this combination with a description of personhood by Wainwright, *The Trinity in the New Testament*, 11.

the Spirit. Because they interact perichoretically, he identifies with the Father and the Spirit and yet is distinguished from them. The Father, Son, and Spirit have a shared life, but the Son is conscious of who he is as a distinct person. This self-consciousness is related to the concept of self-transcendence, a capacity intimately related to the imagination in one's capacities of personhood. A person can stand outside of himself and evaluate himself.

So a person has animate life, which includes consciousness of reality, self-consciousness of one's own identity, and self-transcendence. Conscious life is related to the *ousia* of the triune God in terms of holiness as separation. One aspect of God's holiness is that he transcends creation; thus, by extension, holiness, which is separation, can be viewed as self-transcendence. This means that the holy God is self-conscious of his own identity, such that, though he experiences *perichoresis* (shared life), he is also aware of a separateness or distinctness of life. So God's holiness is the overarching attribute that makes possible the separateness of the persons within the triune Godhead. Holiness is fundamental to the relational nature of the holy Trinity.

THE HEART: FUNCTIONAL CAPACITIES OF PERSONHOOD

There are four capacities in which persons function. In the Old Testament, they are covered by the Hebrew concept of *heart* (*lēb*), and they are clearly evident in the life of Jesus: reason, imagination, emotions, and will.

Reason

A thinking person is the embodiment of reason. Reason includes the logic (rules of correct thinking), memory (things impressed upon the mind from the past), and language (verbal communication between persons). Language is the external evidence of the internal phenomena of logic and memory, all of which are included under the rubric of reason. Jesus obviously used language in his speaking and teaching, giving evidence of clear thinking and memory. The

Gospel of John describes Jesus as the Word (*logos*) of God, who existed before the creation of the universe. This is a clear indication that within the Godhead rational communication is a part of who God is.

For centuries many in the church followed Boethius' definition of a person: "an individual substance of a rational nature." While Boethius accurately discerned a key component of being a person, his definition is not broad enough. The intellect is a key to distinguishing between persons and animals, but other factors are involved.

This is true in the divine nature as well. Jesus has a mind that gives clear evidence of reason at work, in his relationship both with human persons and with the Father and the Spirit. But there is more to understanding personhood than reason.[13]

Imagination

Imagination is closely connected with reason and involves self-transcendence; it allows a person to envision something that is distinct from what a thing is (or could be) in reality. It is a person's capacity to project in his or her mind something that is not yet in existence. For human persons it is envisioning something in the future; for divine persons, unlimited by time, it focuses on that which is possible but has not yet come to be.[14]

Jesus demonstrated his own imagination by envisioning what God intends to do, first in his own life and then in the lives of disciples. When he looked ahead to the cross, to the pouring out of the Holy Spirit, and to the work of the disciples in fulfilling the Great Commission, he was using his imagination. Within the Godhead

---

13. Boethius' definition is also problematic in that a person is viewed as an *individual* instead of in relationship to other persons (see Gunton, *The Promise of the Trinitarian Theology*, 94).

14. For a helpful description of the variety of ways in which the term "imagination" may be used, see Greene, *Imagining God*, 62–66. In spite of his helpful treatment of imagination, Greene appears to want imagination to be the constituent of personhood, replacing the role reason played for Boethius.

itself, this capacity stands behind the creation of the world. First, the triune God imagines its possible existence and then moves to create the world as we know it.

Emotions

The affective side of persons may be described as emotions or feelings. All person-to-person relationships involve some emotion, and this is true with regard to Jesus' personal interaction with others as well. Jesus clearly demonstrates the emotions of anger (John 2:13–16; Mark 11:15–19), love (Mark 10:21), sorrow (Luke 19:41), anguish (Mark 13:34), and joy (John 15:10–12; 16:24). So Jesus expressed the whole realm of personal emotions, which parallels God's emotional expressions toward the people of the Old Testament. In light of Scripture, any attempt to describe God as impassible, meaning he is incapable of emotion, is problematic.

Will

The will, the capacity to choose, is obviously a significant part of personhood. All of Jesus' actions were determined by his choices. Clearly, a volitional element lies behind his choices, even though Jesus repeatedly states that he has aligned his will with that of the Father (John 6:38). This indicates that his will does not belong to him alone but also to his Father. This is a component of divine personhood that becomes central for human persons.

Moral Capacity/Conscience

We have seen that a person is a social being with conscious life and certain functional capacities. Not surprisingly, this combination produces a moral capacity within persons, which encompasses both a conscience and a will. The conscience arises out of one's separateness (self-transcendence), the ability to stand over oneself and evaluate oneself morally and ethically. The conscience requires the use of reason, imagination, and emotion. These three are essential for the sense of moral oughtness, or awareness of right and wrong, that is at the heart of the conscience. Conscience presupposes the capacity to choose between alternatives that reason, imagination, and emotions bring to the person. Conscience is the capacity for knowing right and wrong and demands the moral exercise of the will.

We see this clearly in Jesus' conversation with his Father in Gethsemane. His self-consciousness makes him aware that he is distinct from his Father. As the Father speaks, Jesus becomes aware—through his reason, imagination, and emotions—of God's will for his life. he story is so powerful because Jesus must choose to match his will with that of his Father's, and in this Jesus models the moral capacity of every person, whether divine or human.

The moral dimension of personhood cannot be reduced to one dimension or capacity (e.g., the will). The true content of moral personhood is love expressing holiness and seen in grace, goodness, truth, righteousness, and purity. And these demand other persons for their expression. Thus they are central to the relational Trinity.

FREEDOM

The components of a person already identified—sociality, life, functional and moral capacity—are intricately related to the concept of freedom. This is particularly true of the functional capacities of personhood. Freedom is closely identified with the will of a person, and volition also presupposes understanding and imagination and is often connected with feelings. Furthermore, the ability to make choices presupposes the freedom of self-determination. This freedom is expressed in the social relationships and moral nature of the triune God in which the three members of the holy God freely relate to each other in love.

Our understanding of the Ontological Trinity's freedom is derived from our awareness of Jesus' freedom. In the New Testament narratives, Jesus' freedom to choose is obvious. Jesus' will is particularly obvious at the beginning and the end of his ministry.

First, in the temptation stories, Jesus chooses the will of God but clearly has the freedom not to do so. Then in the garden of Gethsemane, Jesus faces the cross and freely chooses to do the will of God, even though he has many reasons (and emotions) to avoid it.

These stories, which bracket Jesus' ministry, reveal his consistent choice to submit to his Father. He always chooses to align his will with the will of God. This is not predetermined by the Father but is freely chosen by the Son (John 6:38). Jesus models freedom for us. In him we see how to make moral choices: how to love, trust, receive truth, care, obey, and deal with temptation.

Jesus' freedom is consistent with the other parts of being a person. His freedom as a divine person does not include the impersonal or unholy. Jesus' freedom is "the effective energy inherent in God by which God is able to do all things consistent with the divine nature."[15] To be fully personal, one must have freedom of the will in self-determination.

CREATIVITY

Personhood also has a creative component. To do anything creatively, one must have some understanding (reason), the ability to imagine something that does not yet exist, and a freedom of will to bring something into being. Creativity is often accompanied by emotions, although emotion does not seem to be as essential as the other elements.

The New Testament reveals that creativity was a part of Jesus' existence in the Ontological Trinity before the creation of the universe. He is identified as participating in creating the universe and, in particular, creating human persons (John 1:3–4; Col. 1:16; Heb. 1:2). But Jesus also demonstrates creativity in personal relationships. An obvious example is the way he put together and trained a band of disciples over a period of three years (John 1:35–51). The variety of methods Jesus used in teaching his disciples demon-

15. Oden, *The Living God*, 90.

strates remarkable creativity. His creativity in both the physical creation and in personal relationships is aptly illustrated in the story of the marriage at Cana (John 2:1–12).

RESPONSIBILITY

Closely connected to creativity is responsibility. Bringing something into existence entails responsibility for it. A person must understand what he is creating, imagine how to care for it, feel some emotion toward his creation, and freely choose to care for it. The freedom that makes moral choices and creativity possible also makes persons responsible for their choices and creations.

Humans are responsible for their physical creations, but more significantly they are responsible for how they relate to other persons. This is exemplified in the life of Jesus. He is not only responsible for sustaining creation (Col. 1:17), but he is also responsible for the body of believers brought into existence through his creative life (Col. 1:18). In the Gospels, after he calls his disciples, he assumes responsibility for them for the three years of his ministry, and after his ascension he continues to care for them through his Spirit (John 16:4–15).

COINHERENT PERSONHOOD: PERICHORESIS

The early church described the unity and diversity of the persons of the Trinity through "perichoresis," a concept that is particularly appropriate for personhood. The members of the Trinity interpenetrate each other; that is, they share life together. Perichoresis, or coinherence, is an expression of their social nature. This shared life stands behind our understanding of God (and other persons) as being in communion.[16]

This *life-sharing* involves the concept of holiness as love. God is love in his Trinitarian essence. Because of this perichoresis, some-

---

16. T. F. Torrance believes *perichoresis* is the key to the early church's development of its onto-relational concept of divine persons that is at the heart of personhood in Trinitarian theology (*Christian Doctrine of God*, 102). See also Zizioulas, *Being as Communion*.

times Scripture gives us glimpses of the three persons of God relating to each other through their reason, imagination, emotion, and will. So Jesus converses (reason) with his Father, envisions (imagines) what the Father is going to bring to pass, expresses feeling (emotion) about what is coming, and chooses to do God's bidding (will). We also see the triune God perichoretically relating to human persons with one mind, one imagination, one emotion, and one will. This allows men and women to reciprocate, relating to God by relating to any one of the three members. When we relate to one, we relate to all three. Perichoresis is a conceptual tool that helps explain how the three persons relate to each other, how they relate to us, and how we relate to them.

THE PERSONAL AND MORAL ATTRIBUTES OF THE HOLY, TRIUNE GOD

We have identified the personal attributes of God in a more extensive way than some in Christian theology because of the growing conviction that personhood lies at the heart of understanding these attributes. One implication is that the personal attributes highlight the moral dimensions of personal relationships. So the personal attributes naturally lead into a consideration of the moral attributes. Because one of the indicators of God's essence is his holiness, we need to examine the relationship of holiness to both the personal and moral attributes.

PERSONAL ATTRIBUTES AND HOLINESS AS BRILLIANCE

Our beginning point in looking at holiness is the Hebrew word qōdeš. One of the possible etymological meanings of qōdeš is "brilliance" or "brightness." This is certainly connected in Scripture with the immediate personal presence of a holy God among his people.[17]

---

17. Coppedge, *Portraits of God*, 134–35.

The prophet Isaiah declares "the whole earth is full of his glory" (Isa. 6:3). Glory, representing God's holy presence, fills the holy of holies of the Tabernacle at Mount Sinai (Ex. 40:34–35) and the Temple at Jerusalem (1 Kgs. 8:11; 2 Chron. 5:14; 7:1–2). The glory of God is sometimes represented by a cloud and sometimes by fire as at Mount Sinai (Ex. 19:9, 16; 24:15) and in Ezekiel's vision (Ezek. 1:4; 3:5, 10:3–4, 19:6, 8).

The physical symbols of cloud and fire represent the immanence of the personal God among his people. When God comes in these powerful ways, he comes to speak. So when God comes to Mount Sinai to offer a covenant to Israel (Ex. 19–20), he brings instructions—the Ten Words—for his people. When his presence comes to the Tabernacle (Ex. 40:34–35) and the Temple (1 Kgs 8), it fills the holy of holies where the Ten Words are kept. When the Holy One of Israel comes, he speaks to his people. The holy God is personal!

The coming of Jesus as the representative of the Trinity is when the holiness of God is fully manifested to the world (Luke 1:35). The disciples of Jesus came to recognize him as the "the Holy One of God" (John 6:69). Having been given one of the most significant Old Testament titles of God, Jesus now represents the fullest expression of God's personal presence among his people.

When Jesus was raised by the Spirit (Rom. 1:4) and ascended into heaven, he poured out the promised Holy Spirit on his disciples (Acts 2:4, 33). Just as Jesus reflects the full personal and moral character of the triune God in the Gospels, so the Holy Spirit after Pentecost also reflects the full presence of the Trinity in creation. Just as God has made his holy presence known through the Son, now he makes it known through the Spirit. The Spirit filled the Twelve, just as he had filled Jesus (Matt. 3:16), to accomplish God's purposes in the world through them just as God had worked through Jesus. Where the Holy Spirit is, the triune God is, as the brilliant presence of God among the people.

Jesus is significant for understanding the implications of God's holy presence in the world. This is part of Jesus' full revelation of the Economic Trinity, which is why we discussed the personal attributes of God in terms of Jesus' life. As part of these personal attributes, Jesus reveals the moral capacity of personhood, which is exercised in freedom. Here the personal attributes of God open the door for understanding the moral attributes of God (i.e., those attributes that are related to choice: will and freedom). They are therefore intimately related to any discussion of moral holiness.

HOLINESS AND THE MORAL ATTRIBUTES OF GOD

The components of moral holiness are love, righteousness, purity, truth, grace, and goodness. The combination of holiness as love, which is express through the other five components, is of particular significance.

HOLINESS AS LOVE

The love of God expressed in the New Testament is built on God's holiness, which is expressed in the Old Testament by the words *hesed* and *āhēb*. The statement "God is love" presupposes God's declaration, "I am holy." Emil Brunner states:

> The holiness which the Bible teaches is the holiness of the God who is love; therefore the truth of the holiness of God is completed in the knowledge of his love. This indissoluble connection between holiness and love is the characteristic and decisive element in the Christian idea of God.[18]

In the order of knowing, love is best understood as an expression of God's holiness. As the biblical data unfold, love becomes more and more prominent.[19] In the New Testament the full expression

---

18. Brunner in *The Christian Doctrine of God* correctly writes, "Thus the holiness of God is the basis of the self-communication which is fulfilled in love" (164).

19. "Hence for him love is a part of the perfection of Yahweh's nature and a basic element in holiness" (Eichrodt, *Theology of the Old Testament*, 1:281).

of God's love is manifested through the person of God's Son. Then the family categories that describe God and our relationship to him come to the fore, and it is possible to arrive at a much more complete understanding of the love of God. Nevertheless, this expanded knowledge of God's love will be fundamentally unsound if it is not pictured against the standard of God's holy character.[20]

In the order of being, Scripture, love, and holiness are so interwoven that it is difficult to determine their sequence. Sometimes it looks as though love is an expression of God's holiness, and at other times as though holiness and love are interwoven within the *ousia* of God. In any case it is clear that these two, or holy love, dominate the other components of God's moral attributes.

HOLINESS AS TRUTH, PURITY, AND GRACE

When Jesus comes as the Holy One of God in the New Testament (John 6:69), he also comes as the Word of God (John 1:1–3). He comes to speak the truth—the truth about God, ourselves, and the world. Truth is always personal in Scripture. The same Hebrew word (*emet*) is used for truth and faithfulness. God's word can be counted as true because he faithfully keeps his word.

Holiness as *purity* is sometimes connected with the concept of fire. This is the case when God comes to purify Isaiah for his mission (Isa. 6:6–7). Fire also appeared on the day of Pentecost when the disciples are filled with the Holy Spirit. Fire symbolizes purification from their self-centered orientation (Acts 2:1–4; see also Acts 15:8–9).[21] God's holiness as purity refers to his "separation from the impurity and sinfulness of the creature, or expressed positively, the clearness in purity of the divine nature."[22] Theologically,

---

20. As Skevington Wood describes it, "The supreme manifestation of holiness is love" (*ZPEB*, 3:183). On love as an expression of holiness, see Beckwith, "Holiness of God," *NSRE*, 5:318; Muilenburg, "Holiness," *IDB* 2:622; Moody, *The Word of Truth*, 104; Procksch, "ἅγιος," *TDNT*, 1:93; McComisky, "qādôsh," *TWOT*, 2:788.

21. Jacob, *Theology of the Old Testament*, 92.

22. Oehler, *Theology of the Old Testament*, 110.

we may say that purity represents God's freedom from self-centeredness; this complements his other-oriented self-giving.

The concept of *grace* must be understood in a twofold way: as the undeserved favor and the empowering work of God. God's grace is expressed toward his people all through Scripture, and nowhere more clearly than at Mount Sinai. There God declares to Moses, "I will have mercy on whom I will have mercy, and I will have compassion on whom I will have compassion" (Ex. 33:19). Israel had already experienced God's grace in their deliverance from the Egyptians. He did not deliver them because they deserved it but out of his undeserved favor. He redeemed them to follow him and to be the people of God—in the incarnation, "and made his dwelling among us . . . full of grace and truth" (John 1:14). Looking at Jesus, we find that grace and truth are two key ingredients of his life.

HOLINESS AS RIGHTEOUSNESS

God's holiness as righteousness is expressed in the standard of right relationships that he gives to his people. Of course, this standard is patterned on the right relationships between members of the Trinity. Right personal relationships are the heart of righteousness. God does not choose some standard of right beyond himself, but righteousness is a part of the very nature of the right relations within the triune God. The righteous law of God is a description of the holy character of God. This law was established at Mount Sinai when God tells Israel he was looking for a holy people. This expression of holiness is worked out in a standard of righteous living (Ex. 19:6). Isaiah captures this connection between holiness and righteousness: "The LORD Almighty will be exalted by his justice, and the holy God will be proved holy by his righteous acts" (Isa. 5:16; see also Ps. 89:14–18).

The new covenant works on the same principle. God is still developing a holy nation (1 Pet. 2:9). Peter challenges Christians to follow the example of Jesus and so "die to sins and live for righteousness" (1 Pet. 2:24).[23]

Understanding righteousness in relation to the Trinity shifts the focus from it being a legal term to it being a relational category. We first perceive righteousness as about interpersonal relationships and only later find these codified in the law. God had been teaching people about right relationships before the law was given at Sinai. So there is a prior relational base for righteousness in the order of knowing as well as the order of being.

From a Trinitarian perspective our understanding of righteousness must begin with how the Father relates to the Son and Spirit, so family language is fundamental to right relations with others. Therefore, righteousness can no longer be understood as only related to the roles of God as Judge or King. The righteous Father is the foundation for interpreting God's role as Judge, not vice versa.

HOLINESS AS GOODNESS

The connection between goodness and holiness begins with the synonymous use of these terms to describe God's holy presence in his temple: "We are filled with the good things of your house, of your holy temple!" (Ps. 65:4). Then, in describing the benefits of God's "holy name," the psalmist includes that which is "good." We are to "bless the LORD," for the Holy One "satisfies you with good things" (Ps. 103:1, 5). Furthermore, in calling all flesh to bless God's holy name forever, he declares that the people will "praise his holy name for ever and ever" (Ps. 145:7). Clearly, goodness is an expression of God's holy name (i.e., his nature).

The giving of God's Holy Spirit is also connected to the goodness of God. When Isaiah extols "the many good things [God] has done for Israel," he describes God as the one who "set his Holy Spirit among them" (Isa. 63:7–14). In the New Testament Luke compares the good gifts of an earthly father with the heavenly Father's gift of

---

23. Leitch, *ZPBD*, 5:105; Brunner, *The Christian Doctrine of God*, 278.

the Holy Spirit (Luke 11:13). The writer of Hebrews also connects goodness with holiness in declaring that God "disciplines us for our good, in order that we may share his holiness" (Heb. 12:10).

God's name is consistently identified with goodness because, as Pope suggests, holiness is "the standard of goodness."[24] Thus the holy nature of God declares what is morally good. "The reason why good is good" is because the holy God is the eternal standard and foundation of all goodness.[25] In Greek philosophy the "good" may be an abstract idea, but in biblical revelation it is personal in nature and its meaning is governed by a holy and loving God.

Jesus declares, "No one is good but God alone" (Mark 10:18; Luke 18:19; Matt. 19:17). Donald Guthrie rightly warns us that "the character of God is such that it is itself the standard that should determine all human notions of goodness. And that goodness flows from the holy essence of God's being."[26] God does not choose good based on some higher standard than himself; rather, what he wills is good because goodness is an expression of his holy being.[27]

SUMMARY OF THE MORAL ATTRIBUTES

Because moral attributes can be exercised only by persons, there is an intimate connection between them and the personal attributes of God. So the three divine persons are related in the Ontological Trinity through love, truth, purity, grace, righteousness, and goodness. The moral attributes are expressed through the Ontological Trinity's perichoretic relationships and then through the Economic Trinity's relationships with human persons.

---

24. Pope, *Compendium of Christian Theology*, 1:333.
25. Pope, *Compendium of Christian Theology*, 1:333.
26. Guthrie, *New Testament Theology*, 108. See also Packer, "Good," *NBD*, 433–34.
27. Lewis, "Attributes of God," *EDT*, 456.

CHAPTER SEVEN

The Relative and Absolute Attributes of the Triune God

TRINITARIAN THEISM EXPANDS OUR understanding of the personal attributes and changes the order of the discussion of the attributes. Traditionally, the attributes discussed first controlled later discussion. In classical theism the absolute attributes (infinity, immensity, eternity, simplicity, and immutability) and the relative (omnipotence, omniscience, and omnipresence) attributes are viewed as primary. Thus God's role as sovereign monarch is the controlling rubric. God's personal and the moral attributes are subordinated under this approach, and their role in understanding the nature of God is minimized.

The Trinitarian approach significantly changes our view by placing the personal and moral attributes first. Now God's sovereignty is seen in a different light. The absolute and relative attributes are governed by God's personal and moral character, which make person-to-person relationships much more important. This shift in perspective recognized all of God's attributes as they function in a different and more biblical manner.

So, how do God's holiness and love relate to the relative and absolute attributes? The best approach is to connect holiness as *power* to God's relative attributes and holiness as *separation* to

God's absolute attributes. Then the love of the holy, triune God informs and controls these other attributes.

HOLINESS AS POWER: THE RELATIVE ATTRIBUTES OF GOD

The relative attributes of God traditionally include God's omnipotence, omnipresence, omniscience (including foreknowledge), and wisdom. These attributes, sometimes called the communicable, operative or postrelational attributes, explain the way God relates to his created order.[1]

OMNIPOTENCE

Throughout Scripture God's holiness is expressed as power. When God delivers Israel from the Egyptians, the "Song of Moses" praises God, who is "majestic in holiness" and whose right hand is "majestic in power" (Ex. 15:6, 11). This power is further evident in Israel's wandering in the wilderness, when they had to be constantly reminded of the Lord's power (Ps. 78:41–42). The prophets declare that "the Holy One" not only creates people but delivers them "by the greatness of his might, and because of his great power and mighty strength" (Isa. 40:25–26). During the time of the exile God declares that he will one day vindicate his holiness before the nations by demonstrating his power to redeem his people from the exile (Ezek. 36:23–24).

The New Testament reveals holiness as power even before the incarnation. In the birth announcement to Mary the angel says, "The Holy Spirit will come on you, and the power of the Most High will overshadow you. So the holy one to be born will be called the Son of God" (Luke 1:35). Mary responds by praising God: "For the Mighty One has done great things for me—holy is his name" (Luke 1:49). The same emphasis is seen in the resurrection. Paul describes Jesus

---

1. Oden, *The Living God*, 50–51.

as the one "who through the Spirit of holiness was appointed the Son of God in power (Rom. 1:4).[2]

When the relationships of the triune God guides our understanding of holiness as power, then power takes on new meaning. Traditionally, power introduces the relative attributes of God, which normally being with omnipotence and then proceed to omnipresence, omniscience, and wisdom. Omnipotence is the controlling attribute, and when it is connected to the concept of God as sovereign King, as it is in classical theism, it implies autocratic, absolute power. This fits well with the Greek philosophical approach, but not with the Bible.

Our understanding of omnipotence is transformed when we begin with the triune God known through his holiness and love. Omnipotence is no longer seen as the absolute power exercised by a monarch. Instead, it is power exercised by three members of the self-giving God who relates to creation in love. This view does not diminish God's power but sets a completely new context for its exercise. Power is now understood in the service of God's self-giving rather than as an imposition of his will.

As a result, God is no longer pictured as an absolute monarch. For example, he does not elect some and condemn others through an arbitrary use of power. Rather, he is the Holy One who in self-giving love uses his power to enable all persons to enter into a relationship with himself. When omnipotence is the primary attribute, then God can arbitrarily elect some and reprobate others. In this classical model, power becomes more significant than holiness exercised in either righteousness or love. But the Trinitarian approach redefines the way power is exercised, and salvation is necessarily reframed.

---

2. For an exaggerated focus on holiness as power, see Otto, *The Idea of the Holy*. Otto attempts to remove both the moral and the rational (and therefore the relational) elements of holiness and concentrates on the overpowering presence that he describes as the *mysterium tremendum*. Otto attempts to find the common ground between ancient Israel's and its neighbors' concept of the holy. For an evaluation of Otto, see Coppedge, *Portraits of God*, 302–3.

Traditionally, the other relative attributes—omnipresence, omniscience, and wisdom—are subordinated to God's exercise of power. From a Trinitarian perspective these attributes are in the service of God's personal and moral attributes, and how he relates to his creation. God's omnipotence is not reduced or undercut but is set in a more biblical and relational framework.

By giving God's personal attributes priority, the role of personal freedom, both divine and human, is elevated without our theology. Because God desires to freely interact with those who bear his image (i.e., personal attributes), then instead of using his power (omnipotence) to control human persons, he uses it to relate personally with them, respecting their freedom. The other three relative attributes are assume a different role. To relate to freely responding persons, God increasingly relies on his omnipresence, omniscience, and wisdom. Because his power is subordinated to the personal and moral attributes, he accomplishes all of his purposes by being continually present and by using his full knowledge and wisdom. His omnipotence is not used to control personal relationships, but the reverse.

OMNIPRESENCE

Just as God's omnipotence is radically transformed in light of his personal and moral attributes, so is his omnipresence. Because God is a spiritual being and not limited by space (he is immense) and time (he is eternal), he may be simultaneously present everywhere present (omnipresent). The Trinitarian perspective helps explain how God through his Spirit can be immediately present throughout the whole universe.

This attribute of omnipresence connects God's transcendence (i.e., separation from the universe) with his immanence in our world of space and time. The supranatural God who created and oversees the universe is not contained in creation, but he nevertheless has the ability to be present in it for his purposes (Ps. 139:7–10).

God's omnipresence makes it possible for him to continue his providential oversight of creation; he preserves it, supports its normal laws of operation, and in particular guides its affairs. God's omnipresence is related to his availability to relate to other persons in a moral way. He exercises power in the providential rule over inanimate and animate creation, but his primary purpose is to interact with persons made in his own image. So the personal attributes of God become a central focus. Thus, God expresses his moral attributes in personal relationships. He shares in the delights as well as the suffering and hurts others. Omnipresence, from the Trinitarian perspective, means God is present everywhere to relate to human persons in all aspects of their lives.

OMNISCIENCE

The triune God's desire to relate to all persons is also closely connected with his omniscience. God's omniscience begins with his perfect knowledge of himself and then extends to all other things. His understanding is infinite (Ps. 147:5). God's infinite mind has intuitive, simultaneous, and perfect knowledge of all that can be known. He is eternally cognizant of the actual, the possible, and the contingent. Divine omniscience spans the past, the present, and the future.

The omniscience of God is inferred from the larger design of Scripture. The Bible opens with the story of creation (Gen. 1–2) and ends with the close of history (Revelation). The Bible reveals that God, who began and will end the world, has a design for and purposes to accomplish in creation. Unlike the cyclical view of time in the ancient Near East, Israel's linear view of time provides the basis for progression in history.

Because is omniscient, he can reliably run the universe: "See, the former things have taken place, and new things I declare; before they spring into being I announce them to you" (Isa. 42:9). Because God is present everywhere, his knowledge extends to all things (Heb. 4:13; Prov. 15:3). God's knowledge is also personal and individual: "You discern my going out and my lying down; you are familiar with all my ways. Before a word is on my tongue you, LORD, know it completely" (Ps. 139:3–4). This is why Jesus can declare that the very hairs of our heads are known to his Father (Matt. 10:30).

God's omniscience even extends to interior motivations: "I know what is going through your mind" (Ezek. 11:5). Thus Paul states that God "searches all things" so he might know all that it contains (1 Cor. 2:10). John confirms this, saying that God "knows everything" (1 John 3:20). God's omniscience is grounded in his personal attributes and is a direct expression of his reason and imagination, which are components of personhood. These include logic, memory, knowledge, and language and are interwoven in such an intricate way that the persons of the Trinity, who perichoretically share the same mind, also share the same knowledge. God's knowledge is grounded in the personal relationships of the triune God. This is one more witness to the personal nature of truth.

Thomas Oden aptly summarizes the classic thinking on God's omniscience:

> God's knowing is said to be (a) eternally actual, not merely possible; (b) eternally perfect, as distinguished from a knowledge that begins, increases, decreases, or ends; (c) complete instead of partial; and (d) both direct and immediate, instead of indirectly reflected or mediated.[3]

OMNISCIENCE AND FOREKNOWLEDGE

God's omniscience carries a special implication for his foreknowledge. If God knows everything, he knows the past, present, and future. This includes the so-called middle knowledge (*scientia media*) or knowledge of all contingent possibilities.[4] Isaiah is particularly strong in using the concept of foreknowledge to distinguish the God of Israel from all other gods. He argues that only the God of Israel can foretell what is to come: "Remember the former

---

3. Oden, *The Living God*, 71.
4. de Molina, *On Divine Foreknowledge*, 164–95.

things, those of long ago; I am God, and there is no other; I am God, and there is none like me. I make known the end from the beginning, from ancient times, what is still to come" (Isa. 46:9–10).

God's ability to do all that he desires to do is based not only on his own decisions but also on his perfect knowledge of the choices and motivations of other persons. To limit God's foreknowledge to the choices that he is going to make, as in open theism,[5] is simply too partial in its description of God's understanding according to Scripture.

Unfortunately, the starting point of the Augustinian, Thomistic, and Calvinistic traditions has been the absolute sovereignty of God. With such a beginning, foreknowledge becomes foreordination. So if God foreknows something, he must have previously ordained it to come to pass. With this view of God's sovereignty, nothing could happen that God has not caused. So God foreknows because he forecauses. But this eliminates human freedom. If God knows what choices human persons will make, then that surely implies (from the classical traditions' perspective) that God has made all the choices. This makes human freedom an illusion.

Open theologians respond by declaring that the Bible clearly supports human freedom, so God's omniscience, and particularly his foreknowledge, must be limited. So foreknowledge is equated with foreordination for the open as well as the classical theists.[6] Open theists escape from this dilemma by opting for freedom and rejecting foreknowledge. But the question arises: Is there another alternative? Here Trinitarian theism serves us well.

Scripture passages that imply God expects persons to respond in freedom confirm the capacity for freedom that all persons, whether divine or human, possess. To be a person means to have freedom of choice. In Scripture, the tri-personned God repeatedly addresses men and women, expecting them to freely respond to his directions

---

5. Boyd, "The Open Theism View," 13–37.
6. Pinnock, *Most Moved Mover*, 84, 107.

and invitations. The key to understanding foreknowledge, then, is to begin with a Trinitarian rather than a classical understanding of God. Within the triune God, the three divine persons have knowledge and freedom, and persons made in God's image have the capacity for both. God may foreknow something that he does not forecause. He may know the free choices of persons without foreordaining those choices.

WISDOM

Wisdom is the practical application of God's omniscience. The coordination of God's knowledge with his infinite ability to bring about his ends is accomplished through his wisdom (Rom. 11:33). Like the other three relative attributes, God's wisdom is closely bound up with his sovereign direction of the universe. The questions of providence have to do with God's use of knowledge in terms of ends and means. God employs his wisdom to apply knowledge for accomplishing his purposes (Job 12:13).

Wisdom is applied knowledge that particularly relates to people in a way that is consistent with God's moral attributes. This confirms that truth in Scripture is never abstract but is always personal in nature. This is why Jesus is the key to understanding how God works in relationship to the world. In him the personal connects with truth, and he illustrates how God in his wisdom providentially desires to relate to all persons.

Finally, Trinitarian theism protects us from the temptation to turn God's knowledge and wisdom into abstractions. Knowledge knowledge's sake is not characteristic of God. Rather, knowledge is designed to be in the service of God's creation in general, and persons in particular. So our focus is on wisdom in personal relationships rather than truth as an abstraction.

Beginning with the Trinity makes God's personal and moral attributes primary and significantly changes our understanding of God's relative attributes. In particular it keeps the exercise of power from being arbitrary, and it brackets the use of power, presence, knowledge, and wisdom within God's relational and moral character.

HOLINESS AS SEPARATION: THE ABSOLUTE ATTRIBUTES OF GOD

Holiness is conceived as separation when the Bible refers to God's transcendence over the world of space and time. God is not part of the natural world but is the supernatural one—the wholly other one (see Hos. 11:9). The Lord's Prayer illustrates this connection between God's holiness and his transcendence. It opens with "Our Father in heaven," which highlights his separateness from the universe. This is immediately followed by the declaration "Hallowed be your name" (Matt. 6:9). He whose name is holy is also the one who transcends the world.

The concept of holiness as separation is highlighted by one of the possible etymologies of the Hebrew word for holy, qōdeš. It may come from the root qd, which means "to divide or separate." This suggests its original meaning may have been "cut off, withdrawn or set apart."[7]

Holiness as separateness points to God as creator. Isaiah makes a strong connection between the holiness of God and his role as transcendent Creator: "This is what the LORD says—the Holy One of Israel, and its Maker: . . . It is I who made the earth and created mankind on it'" (Isa. 45:11–12; 54:5; 17:7). The same picture appears at the close of Scripture where the enthroned God is worshiped as "holy, holy, holy" by the creatures who also declare, "for you created all things, and by your will they were created and have their being" (Rev. 4:8, 11).

God existed as triune from the beginning. Accordingly, his personal nature as Father is prior to his role as Creator. The personal

---

7. Snaith, *The Distinctive Ideas of the Old Testament,* 24–25; Coppedge, *Portraits of God,* 54–57.

and moral attributes of God are determinative in understanding how God creates and relates to the world he transcends.[8] When the concepts of God's holiness and love are emphasized, the absolute attributes cannot be divorced from these aspects of God's being.

The absolute attributes of God normally refer to those components of who God is within himself apart from how he relates to the created universe. These primary, or essential, attributes are sometimes referred to as incommunicable, quiescent, or prerelational.[9] These absolute attributes of a transcendent, triune, holy God include his spirituality, infinity, self-sufficiency, and constancy.

SPIRITUALITY

Jesus clearly describes God as spirit in John 4:24. Traditionally, God's spirituality has three components: unity, simplicity, and incorporeality. In light of a Trinitarian context for understanding the attributes, a fourth category must be added: personhood.

The *unity of God* is based on the monotheism of the Bible; it focuses on the oneness of his triune essence (Isa. 45:5, 7, 11–12, 18; Deut. 4:39). The great Shema, "Hear, O Israel: the LORD our God, the LORD is one" (Deut. 6:4, Mark 12:29), is echoed by the New Testament doxology, "to the King of eternal, immortal, invisible, the only God" (1 Tim. 1:17). Both Testaments teach that "there is one God" (1 Tim. 2:5, 1 Cor. 8:6). But the unity of God, so clearly unfolded in the order of knowing in the Old Testament, takes on a different cast in light of the revelation of the triune nature of God in the New. While God does not cease to be one, three persons share one essence. This means there is a triunity within the nature of the Godhead. He cannot be divided into parts, but neither can he be considered a monad. So the relational nature of the triune God qualifies our concept of unity.

---

8. Pope proposes we cannot understand absolute attributes without first understanding the personal attributes, which in turn can only be understood in light of the Trinity (*Compendium of Christian Theology*, 1:306–7).

9. Oden, *The Living God*, 50–51.

The *simplicity of God* means he is not divisible into parts. Throughout church history simplicity has meant that God is not a composite being; he is one. Therefore all of God is present in all of his activities. Theologians employ the term "perichoresis" to describe how the members of the Trinity can be one God. While he is not divisible into parts, he is three persons with one essence. So while a triune understanding of simplicity guards against focusing solely on the oneness of God, it also protects Christian theology against tritheism.

God's spirituality also means he is immaterial and invisible, or *incorporeal*. This distinguishes God from the created and material universe. When the Scriptures teach that God is pure spirit, it means that he does not have a literal body (John 4:24). Paul reinforces this, declaring God to be immortal and invisible (1 Tim. 1:17). God cannot be identified with any single part of the natural creation. Rather, he is the transcendent Creator who is discontinuous with the physical universe of space and time.

This does not mean that God may not at times choose to enter the universe and take on physical form, such as when he appeared to Abraham (Gen. 18). Further, God may be described in an anthropomorphic manner. But these physical descriptions of God (e.g., God's arm) are not to be understood literally. They are metaphorical language to assist our understanding of how God works.

Our Trinitarian perspective also qualifies our understanding of God's incorporeality. With the incarnation, we believe God assumed a human form, becoming visible and corporeal. While he remains a spiritual being, his incarnation broadens our understanding of his simplicity. God's assumption of human nature through the Second Person of the Trinity ensures that there is no dualism between God's transcendence and immanence. He has entered creation and experienced material existence in human form, and however mysterious this is, God has sovereignly chosen to let this experience have a permanent effect upon himself. It further allows humans, who only know personhood in a corporeal way, to know and relate to God through his incarnate Son. This certainly changes our concept of and relationship to God.

God's personhood, part of his spiritual nature, helps explain the second commandment, which forbids the creation of any material image of God. God cannot be identified with creaturely matter, but he is represented within the created order by human persons made in his own image. "God is not matter" is a part of the definition of God as spirit. Human persons, who embody spirituality in their own personhood, represent the spiritual nature of the invisible and incorporeal God.

INFINITY AND ETERNALITY

The infinity of God's divine nature means that he is without bounds or limits. He is a supranatural being who is outside of both time and space. Infinity thus has a twofold reference point: first, God is *eternal*; second, God is *immense*.

The eternity of God (i.e., infinity in relationship to time) means God is without beginning or end; he stands outside of time.[10] He is the great and timeless "I AM." Thus, he is described as the first and the last (Isa. 41:4; 44:6). He is the everlasting God (Isa. 40:28; Ps. 90:2). In the New Testament, John speaks of grace and peace from "him who is and who was and who is to come" (Rev. 1:4). The Lord God declares of himself, "I am the Alpha and the Omega . . ." (Rev. 1:8). Further, Jude describes Jesus as "before all time, now, and forevermore" (Jude 25).

Whereas the eternity of God has to do with infinity in relationship to time, God's immensity is his infinity in relationship to space. God is not limited or circumscribed by space anymore than he is by time; he transcends both: "The heavens, even the highest heaven cannot contain you" (1 Kgs. 8:27; 2 Chron. 6:18). Though God transcends space, he also may come into the universe without

---

10. For a discussion of several views of time, see Ganssle, *God and Time*.

being localized or identical with any particular part of it (Isa. 40:22; 66:1; Jer. 23:24; Deut. 4:39; Ps. 139:7). God's immensity implies his omnipresence. Beginning with the order of being, it is God's immensity that makes possible his omnipresence. God's lack of spatial limitation makes it possible for him to simultaneously accomplish his purposes throughout all of creation.[11]

God has chosen not only to share his personal life but also his love with persons in his creation. He relates especially to the personal part of the created world, even though he is clearly seen as distinct and separate from it. So the attribute of God's infinity helps maintain the distinction between the divine and the created (especially the human) while at the same time allowing for a relationship between God and human persons. This connection expresses God's personal and loving nature, which gives rise to his creation of a world with which he can share life and love.

Theologically, infinity elevates the supernatural character of God and protects us from pantheism (all is God) or panentheism (all is a part of God). In contrast to the rest of the ancient Near Eastern world, the God of the Bible is never identified with our world. He is separate and distinct from it. Today in much Eastern philosophy and theology, the line between the divine and created is blurred. In the contemporary West, pantheism and panentheism thrive in new forms such as New Age thought and process theology.

How does an infinite God relate to a creation from whom he is distinct? First, he does so by revelation. He makes himself known through the created order (general revelation) as well as through his rational communication (special revelation). So the triune God, who is a personal being, communicates to created persons through all the faculties of personhood that make such communication possible. This again places God's personal attributes in the midst of his absolute attributes.

---

11. Oden, *The Living God*, 61.

This connection between the Creator and creation is completed and personalized with the coming of the Second Person of the Trinity in the incarnation. Here the triune God forever weds himself to the created world so there is a bridge between the infinite and the finite, from the Creator to the creation. This does not blur the distinction between the divine and the created or between God and humanity, but it unites the two in the person of Jesus, the God-Man. The infinite, supernatural God entered the natural world of space and time and provided a permanent connection between the two without blurring the discontinuity between them. Our Trinitarian theism, then, balances God's infinity with his presence in creation, his transcendence and his immanence.

SELF-SUFFICIENCY

The third absolute attribute of God is his self-sufficiency. This is sometimes described as his *aseity* or his *self-subsistence*, meaning that he possesses life in himself. God is not dependent upon anyone or anything outside of himself for his own existence. God has no external cause; he simply and eternally *is*. All existence and life find their cause in him. This is surely part of what God had in mind when he revealed his name to Israel as "I AM WHO I AM" (Ex. 3:14). Thus he declared, "Before me no god was formed, nor will there be anyone after me" (Isa. 43:10) and "I am he; I am the first, and I am the last" (Isa. 48:12; see also Gen. 1:1; Isa. 44:6). He alone is uncreated and the underived source of all (Ps. 90:1–4).

This self-existence of God means that there is nothing above or beyond God that is responsible for his existence. The contrast is particularly clear in comparing the God of Israel to the gods of the ancient Near Eastern world. In a pagan worldview, above and beyond the gods was a concept of the metadivine, which may be variously described as a force, fate, or primeval stuff. It was responsible for the gods' existence. But the God of Scripture is not part of he natural order nor is there any force, fate, or metadivine above or

HOLY LOVE: A WESLEYAN SYSTEMATIC THEOLOGY

beyond him. He exists only with himself, and he is solely responsible for all other things.

The relationship of God's self-existence to his personal and moral attributes centers in the Trinitarian nature of his being. While nothing can be above or beyond God, there is an interrelatedness within himself. So, in the Godhead self-existence is not that of a single individual but of a triune relationship. The three members of the Godhead actively give themselves to one another. Understanding the priority of God's personal attributes, expressed in the three divine persons' self-giving love, removes any temptation to think of God before creation as either a monad or some impersonal force out of which everything else emerged. Rather, in his triune being there is "infinite variety of life, in the mutual knowledge, love, and communion of the Father, the Son, and the Holy Ghost."[12]

Constancy

The fourth of the absolute attributes is God's reliability. This refers to the fact that there is no essential change in any attribute of God's nature. As the Psalmist declares, "But you remain the same, and your years will never end" (Ps. 102:27). The Lord declares of himself, "I the LORD do not change" (Mal 3:6). Jesus, who is the full reflection of the Father, is described as "the same yesterday and today and forever" (Heb. 13:8). The unchangeableness of God is our guarantee that the one we trust today will not be different tomorrow. Our faith is built on the trustworthiness and sameness of God's character.[13]

Classical theists usually describe this attribute as "immutability," defining it in terms of absolute changelessness. If God changes, they argue, he could not be a perfect being. Change implies he could become more or less perfect, which is an impossibility. Because God is the only perfect being, change must be excluded. A third option

---

12. Pope, *Compendium of Christian Theology*, 1:301.
13. While some of the descriptions of God's work in terms of his various roles seem to imply changes in him (God *repented* of an action), this is not to be understood in terms of a change in his essence, attributes, purposes, or character.

remains, however. Change for God is just different; it does not imply either more or less perfection as it might in reference to creation. But some theologians make God's immutability such that he never changes at all, either in his relationships or in himself.

From the Trinitarian perspective, God's unchangeableness must be understood in personal terms, where freedom and choice are an integral part of what is being described. No personal relationships are static; they are all dynamic. Person-to-person relationships cannot be frozen; they adjust or change in some respects. Because our relationship with God changes, it has some kind of effect on him and us.[14]

In light of this, the biblical passages that imply God's constancy must be understood in regard to his personal and moral attributes. The personal nature of his being is not going to change. Likewise, his character and his purposes both for himself and for the world are not going to change. But the relationship between God and other persons change in some respects, depending on their responses to him. Because God is reliably the same, he can adjust to to the change that occurs within persons, relations, and history. This account of immutability is consistent with the biblical record of the faithful God who is always the same in his character, nature, and purpose.

This Trinitarian approach to divine constancy carries with it several implications. First, God's essential being is not "developing" as suggested by Process Theology. God's purposes and character as well as his essence are not changing in some new way. Second, from a Trinitarian perspective, this approach to God's unchangeableness allows for dynamic and interactive relationships between God and human persons. This sets the context for understanding the few passages about God "repenting" of his actions. Third, this approach also allows for the significant change that comes with the incarnation. While God's purposes, character, and essential nature do

---

14. Oden does not place this attribute under the absolute attributes but under the moral attributes because it must not be divorced from God's moral and relational character (*The Living God*, 110–11).

not change in the incarnation, some change certainly takes place. At the incarnation God forever weds himself to his creation in a unique way by taking on human form. So thought the Son of God experiences change—coming into the world, living, dying, rising, ascending, and waiting for a second return—it is a very qualified and nuanced change that reveals rather than alters his character, purposes, and essential nature.

This Trinitarian perspective facilitates understanding the Scriptures that describe God as "repenting."[15] Do these passages imply a change in God's basic attributes, character, or purposes? No. These Scriptures speak in an anthropomorphic way to describe God's response to human persons; that is, they speak of God as if he were another human being changing in a relationship. A supranatural God of course knows what he is going to do and how others are going to respond all along. But he condescends to relate to us in an easily understood (human) way; thus we describe him using human categories such as "changing his mind." Understanding these few passages (and there are only a few) in this light is far more satisfactory than ignoring the massive biblical data that supports God's foreknowledge, which controls his own actions and his governance of the world. Rejecting God's foreknowledge in order to explain God's "changing his mind" is a bit like straining out a gnat and swallowing a camel! By placing the accent on God's personal attributes we strengthen our understanding of his constancy in responding to people, and this makes it possible to understand these passages without falling into the foreknowledge-denying trap of open theism.[16]

---

15. Gen. 6:6, 7; Ex. 32:14; 1 Sam. 15:35; Jer. 26:3, 13, 19; Amos 7:3; Jonah 3:10.
16. For further discussion, see Richards, *The Untamed God,* and Roy, *How Much Does God Foreknow?*.

THE NATURE OF THE TRIUNE GOD

One of the benefits of a triune approach to understanding the nature of God is that it holds together the biblical data on both the transcendence and the immanence of God. The triune God, who created the universe and stands outside of space and time, enters creation in the person of the Son. This protects us, on the one hand, from making God so transcendent that he seems unconcerned with the world, and, on the other hand, it guards us from the kind of immanence that identifies God with the world.

The Trinitarian approach addresses the concern of classical theism to preserve the sovereignty of God. God the Creator has made a world of which he is not a part but over which he rules. However, the Trinitarian approach redefines God's sovereignty by shifting the focus from God as King to God as Father. So God's sovereignty is not first connected with majesty and power but with personal and family relationships. Because God is Father within the Ontological Trinity, he is able to assume the role of Father to human persons, especially to those persons who enter into an appropriate relationship with him.

This also addresses the concern of open theism that classical theism has made God too remote and distant from his people, especially in their pain and suffering. But a father is intimately involved in the life of his family, and the coming of the Son on behalf of the Father through the power of the Spirit is the way the triune God identifies himself with his children. In fact, Jesus' interaction with persons in his own day is the living illustration of how the triune God desires to interact with persons of every generation. This shift to a Trinitarian view of God is a more adequate response to the open theism critique than the suggestion that we need a more compassionate king.[17]

---

17. Feinberg, *No One Like Him,* 701.

Trinitarian Theism balances God's transcendence and immanence. The triune God certainly transcends the world he has created. But the advent of Jesus binds God to his people in a graphic and permanent way. God clearly desires not only to relate to his people but also to identify with them. In Jesus he identifies with every component of human lives: relationships with families, friends, government, culture, etc. God is concerned about pain and suffering in our sinful, fallen world, which became obvious in Jesus' life, death, and resurrection. In light of this, the abstract concept of impassability must be drastically revised. The triune God does identify with suffering and even participates in it. The older view that Jesus suffered only in his human nature simply is not adequate; it disregards the biblical data and the theological implications of the triune God who comes into the world. Because all of life is a gift from God, he not only identifies with pain, hurt, and suffering but also with joy and delight in the fullness of the experiences of life, family, growth, knowledge and so on.

CHAPTER EIGHT

The Roles of the Triune God
The Way the Economic Trinity Works

HOW DO WE KNOW THE SUPRANATURAL GOD?

BECAUSE THE TRIUNE GOD is a supranatural being and ordinary human perception is limited to the natural world, how is it possible for people to know God? Can humans comprehend a God who is who is outside the world of space and time? Human language is necessarily confined to the world of creation. Recognizing our dilemma (particularly the finite nature of our perception), God has condescended to use human language to describe his own transcendent being. Working with terms from creation, and particularly from personal relations, God tells us what he is like.[1]

The best way to describe the transcendent God is by use of *analogical language* (i.e., using terms that are alike in some but not all ways).[2] So, for example, from the natural world we understand what

---

1. "A human knowledge of God can be a true knowledge that corresponds to the divine reality only if it originates in the Deity itself. God can be known only if he gives Himself to be known" (Pannenberg, *Systematic Theology*, 1:1); Brunner, *The Christian Doctrine of God*, 118. See also Coppedge, *Portraits of God*, 21–38.

2. On analogy see Aquinas, *Summa Theologica*, vol. 1, Q.13; *Summa Contra Gentiles,* 1:32–34; Mascall, *Existence and Analogy,* 92–121; Sherry, "Analogy Reviewed" and "Analogy Today": 337–45, 431–46.

power is, and that assists us (by comparison) to understand God's work as all-powerful (almighty) or omnipotent. So by *analogy* the use of *power* in relation to God is similar to our use of *power* in this world. But it is also dissimilar; "power" is often impersonal, as in the power of electricity. So God is connected with power in his omnipotence, but he is not a mere force—an impersonal power.

There are many kinds of analogies. For our purposes, the one that has particular relevance is *metaphor*. Aristotle aptly captured the significance of metaphor: "If one wants to master speech, one must master metaphor."[3] A metaphor is a specialized form of analogical language in which one thing (a subject) is compared to another (a symbol). When God is described using metaphors, there is an analogy between God (the subject) and something in the created world (the symbol) that is based on the similarity of being, action, or relationship. When the Psalmist calls God a "rock" (Ps. 32:1, 2) he is using a metaphor to help us understand that God is unchanging and provides a firm foundation for whatever we do.

The metaphors that imply the greatest degree of correspondence between God and the symbol from this world are those that are taken from personal relations. This kind of "human" metaphor for God may be called a *role*. These roles (a metaphor itself borrowed from the theater) indicate truths about God by comparing him to the way human persons act and relate to others. Each of these indicates that this is the way God *is*, this is the way God *acts*, and this is the way God *relates to others*. The use of these role metaphors allows the Bible to graphically depict God as King, Father, or Judge.[4] The metaphorical roles are the primary description of the way the Economic Trinity relates to creation.

---

3. Paul, "Metaphor," in *Dictionary for Theological Interpretation for the Bible*, 507.

4. See Richard Baukham's use of "The Identity of God" as an alternative label in *God Crucified*, 7–8. John Frame refers to them under the images of God in *The Doctrine of God*, 368–78.

Role is the primary term we are going to use to describe these personal images of God, while *metaphor, analogy, portrait*, and *identity* will be used as secondary terms.[5] G. B. Caird points out that these roles/metaphors derived from human relationships have special significance because they work as a two-way traffic in ideas:

> When the Bible calls God Judge, King, Father or Husband it is, in the first instance using the human known to throw light on the divine unknown. But no sooner has the metaphor traveled from earth to heaven than it begins the return journey to earth, bearing with it an ideal standard by which the conduct of human judges, kings, fathers and husbands is to be assessed.[6]

Caird's valuable insight is that while God draws from this world to describe himself, when we understand his full revelation, the metaphors are reshaped by God's own being and become the standard for a new understanding of human roles. God is the model for the way each role is intended to describe the way God desires to relate to his creation.

God uses multiple roles/metaphors because none is fully adequate in itself. In addition, because no human judge, king, or father is ideal, our perception of these roles is often distorted. Yet enough is known about each of these human roles to give us a better understanding of some aspect of the nature of God.

It is true that a proper understanding of God's roles must be corrected in light of a larger understanding provided by Scripture. One of the major problems in the history of the church may be the tendency of different segments of the church to emphasize certain roles. When one or two roles are accentuated, an unbalanced picture of God results. Because incomplete as well as distorted views

---

5. Three kinds of metaphors are used for God: inanimate objects (God is a rock), animals (the Lion of the tribe of Judah), and persons (King, Father, Shepherd). On a scale of increasing comparison, the inanimate objects are clearly where the comparison is least like God, and the personal metaphors are the ones that are most like him.

6. Caird, *The Language and Imagery of the Bible*, 19.

of God ultimately lead to a stunted or imbalanced Christian experience, a more complete understanding of the triune God will hopefully lead us to a deeper personal knowledge of God. God's nature is not separable or neatly divisible, and so the biblical passages that mix these roles come as a healthy corrective to our analytic treatment of them.

THE ROLES OF THE TRIUNE GOD

The chief focus of God as *Personal Revealer*, for example, is that of fellowship and communication of truth in interpersonal relationships. The term "Personal Revealer" indicates a role of the Economic Trinity. The source of all divine action is the tripersonal life of God.[7] All three persons of the Economic Trinity work in all the roles. In our survey of the biblical evidence underlying the doctrine of the Trinity, we noted that all three persons work in all eight major roles. Although in terms of their titles, a particular divine person may be identified with a specific role, all three members do the same activity in each of the eight roles. Seeing all three persons in all eight roles broadens our understanding of the Trinitarian nature of God.

PERSON OF CHRIST

Christology is connected with the Old Testament by the fact that all of the roles of God revealed under the old covenant are more vividly expressed in the person of Christ. The roles Jesus plays under the new covenant parallel each of those Yahweh demonstrated about himself under the old covenant. By this parallel use of roles for God and for Jesus, the identity of God is given fresh meaning and clearer illustration.[8] Because of the union of the divine with the human (the

---

7. These eight major roles of God do not exhaust the personal biblical metaphors; others may be understood as subcategories of these eight. For a chart of sub-roles and a more extensive discussion, see Coppedge, *Portraits of God,* 27–29.

8. See Baukham, *God Crucified,* 6–13.

theandric union) in Jesus, he demonstrates more clearly both who God is and God's design for human beings. Thus Jesus, in the creation metaphor, is not only the Creator of the cosmos and the image of God but also the image of the perfect human being. Similarly, he is the King of the universe and also the Servant of God. He reveals God as the divine Word, frequently as a Prophet and Teacher. But in his humanity he models friendship with God, cultivating a relationship by listening to him in prayer and being receptive to all God has to say.

Jesus serves as the High Priest while also modeling a perfect sacrifice. As God he is Judge, but he also models perfect obedience to the law. In familial terms, Jesus is the Son of God as well as the Son of Man. In his divinity, he is the good Shepherd, while in his humanity he shows us how to follow God.

PERSON OF THE HOLY SPIRIT

A parallel case can be made for understanding the Holy Spirit. One of the Spirit's major responsibilities is to call attention to the Father and to the Son rather than to himself (John 16:13–15). The descriptions of the Spirit are certainly less vivid than the way the roles describe the Father and the Son.

However, an examination of the data reveals that in terms of *function*, the Spirit's work parallels all eight roles of the Father and the Son. In the Old Testament, the "Spirit of God" works in all the roles that God does, which prepares us for the fuller revelation in the New Testament. Just as the incarnation makes more vivid the several roles of God the Father (John 1:18), so too Jesus brings alive the roles of the Spirit.

In terms of God's economic activity, the Spirit plays a role of Creator in Genesis, and then he is the ruling presence of the Godhead in the lives of the believers (King). He is also the Spirit of truth who makes God's revelation possible in this world (Personal Revealer). The Spirit intercedes for people (Priest), and he serves as the Counselor and Advocate for them before God (Judge). At the same time he is the agent of the new birth that brings us into God's family (Father). The Spirit empowers people to serve God (Redeemer), and he gives direction to the lives of individuals (Shepherd).

The Spirit's work can only be understood in light of all these categories. No analogy or role from this world will be perfectly adequate to explain the transcendent God. There is always a component of mystery in knowing God. This is one of the reasons why so many different analogies are used. The various roles condition one another and help us see God more perfectly.

THE TRINITY AND FOUNDATIONAL ROLES

The analogical language of the roles may be divided into two types: metaphysical and metaphorical. While the former applies to the very being of God, the latter do not. A metaphysical analogy has to do with the essence of God's *being*, whereas a metaphorical analogy describes the way God *works* in relationship to others. The former relates to the Ontological Trinity, and the latter primarily to the Economic Trinity. We have mainly discussed the metaphorical roles used of the Economic Trinity: Creator, King, Priest, Judge, Redeemer, and Shepherd. Now we will look at the metaphysical analogy and the two major roles associated with it: God as Personal Revealer and God as Father.

Metaphysics has to do with the essence or being of something. Like the metaphorical analogies, God is like a Personal Redeemer and a Father in some ways but unlike them in other ways. The added metaphysical dimension in these two roles corresponds to the inner being of the triune God; an important dimension of his essence is revealed in a way that is not so with the purely metaphorical roles.

As Personal Revealer the members of the Trinity relate to each other within one Ontological Trinity. The personal relationships and communication within the Trinity are central to the very essence or being of God. The same is true of the relationship between the

Father and the Son. Classic Christian theology understands this distinction between the Father and the Son: one begets and the other is eternally begotten. Thus there was fatherhood in the Ontological Trinity before it was expressed toward us in the Economic Trinity.

Because *Personal Revealer* and *Father* have to do with the basic essence of God's nature, there is a sense in which God is more like these two roles than any of the others. These roles more accurately and more fully describe who God is as well as the way he works. We could refer to them as foundational roles for the Christian faith. When their priority is taken seriously, it has profound implications for the rest of our theology. For example, when we begin with God's personal nature and his fatherhood, rather than God's role as Creator or King, these become the heart of our perception of God. This has very practical implications for how God relates to our world.

This understanding of God also affects the order of his attributes. The centrality of God as *Father* means that God expresses himself as a God of love. Love, previously understood as one component of God's holiness, now is pushed to the forefront. The holy, triune God expresses himself through six moral attributes, but God's self-giving love, which is most characteristic of the inner nature of the Trinity, is dominant. So the metaphysical significance of the role of God as Father is that God's love is connected with his holiness, and these two attributes control his other attributes.

The conclusion is that the God who makes himself known in the Economic Trinity (*opera ad extra*) is the same God within himself that we call the Ontological Trinity (*opera ad intra*). Because he is the same triune God, there is a correspondence between who he is in his action toward us *(pro nobis)* and who he is in his being *(in se)*.

CHAPTER NINE

The Triune God's Work of Providence

THE FUNCTION OF PROVIDENCE

THE DOCTRINE OF PROVIDENCE examines and explains the interaction between the triune Creator and his creation. A Trinitarian view of providence protects Christians against several erroneous views of God's work within creation: deism, pantheism, fatalism, and chance.

Deism, which primarily views God as Creator, severely limits his interaction with the world once it is complete. God's transcendence so dominates deism that he is virtually separated from creation's ongoing operation. Deism's Creator is like a watchmaker who winds up a watch and then leaves it to run on its own. Though deism begins with supranaturalism, it ends with practical naturalism. The biblical concept of providence counters this view by showing that God has not left it to run its own course. He interacts with his creation by sustaining it, preserving it, caring for it, and governing its operations. The biblical doctrine of providence is a healthy antidote to a deistic worldview.

The biblical doctrine of providence also counters *pantheism*. Pantheism is the identification of God with the created order itself.

Here all things are God. Whereas the God of deism is totally transcendent, pantheism's God is completely immanent. The biblical view of providence addresses the pantheistic option by revealing the transcendent Creator who interacts with his creation without being identified with any of its parts. Biblically, God is transcendent and immanent.

Fatalism teaches that things are absolutely predetermined, either by impersonal fate or by a supranatural God who has predetermined all the choices and events of creation. Either way, the practical effect of fatalism is the same: it undercuts human freedom and responsibility. The biblical doctrine of providence demonstrates that God relates to persons who make free and spiritually significant choices. A scriptural view of providence undercuts the ground of fatalism.

That life is based on pure *chance* is a variation of fatalism. According to this view, everything is the result of the impersonal plus time plus chance. Things happen without plan or purpose; life is truly random. The concept of providence makes it clear that the world does not operate by chance. Providence declares that life is not purposeless but has God-designed purpose and meaning, and that significance is found in fellowship with the triune God.

The doctrine of providence not only addresses errors regarding the doctrine of God, it also speaks to two major issues that arise in every generation: theodicy and miracles. The doctrine of providence also has enormous pastoral implications. Thinking Christians cannot help but ask how God is working in their personal lives, their families, their churches, their nations, and the world. They want to know how God works and how this affects them and others.[1]

---

1. Grudem, *Systematic Theology*, 315; Brunner, *The Christian Doctrine of Creation and Redemption*, 148; Nigel M. de S Cameron, "Providence," *NDT*, 541–42; Oden, *The Living God*, 277–78.

THREE COMPONENTS OF PROVIDENCE

The doctrine of providence is traditionally divided into three interrelated parts: the work of God in sustaining his creation (*preservation*), the way God cooperates with natural and secondary causes to run the universe in an orderly fashion (*concurrence*), and how God governs all things, including free agents, to accomplish his purposes (*governance*). These three concepts under the term "providence" are related to root meanings from the Greek *pronoia* and the Latin *pro-videre*—both meaning *to see ahead* or *to anticipate*. The concept of providence is about God's ability to foresee what will be needed in his creation and provide for the needs of the world.[2]

PRESERVATION

Preservation is God's work of maintaining, upholding, and sustaining his creation (Ps. 138:7). Two Bible texts reveal the intimate connection between the triune God and this work of preservation. Both come in christological sections. In Colossians 1:15–19 Jesus is described as "the image of the invisible God" through whom all things were created. In Hebrews 1:1–5 Jesus is presented as the Son of God through whom God "also created the universe" and who continues "sustaining all things by his powerful word."

As Creator, God is the prime cause of all things, but his work of preservation is carried out through multiple secondary causes. When God created the cosmos, he set the laws of cause and effect in place, and he works through these to maintain his creation.

Among the secondary causes is the gift of human free will. God's providence does not exclude the will but works through it and sus-

---

2. For variations on the ordering of these components and providence, see: Pope, "Conservation, Care and Governance," in *A Compendium of Christian Theology*, 1:437ff; and Gunton, "Conservation, Governance, Perfecting, Rest," in *The Triune Creator*, 176f. Using this traditional order are Oden, *The Living God*, 270–73; Grudem, *Systematic Theology*, 315; Pannenberg, *Systematic Theology*, 2:35–59; Barth, *Church Dogmatics* 3/3, 313, 58–238.

tains it. Even after the Fall, God by his prevenient grace sustains the human capacity to make free choices.[3]

The preservation of God's creation like the other parts of the work of providence, is based on his omnipresence, which allows him to know the state of everything in the world, his wisdom (including omniscience), and his power (omnipotence), which allows him bring about what his goodness determines is best for his creatures.[4]

Concurrence

Divine concurrence means God's providential cooperation with secondary causes as his basic means of caring for the created world. In the order of causality, God is the primary cause of all things, but he has created a world in which there are also secondary causes that operate in the natural, rational, and moral dimensions of life. The doctrine of concurrence focuses on God's continuous work through secondary causes, sustaining them and using them to accomplish his purposes for each kind of created being.[5]

The doctrine of concurrence has particular significance for humans. By sharing he triune God's personal attributes, they possess reason, imagination, emotions, and will along with corresponding freedom, responsibility, and creativity. God maintains the same human capacities with which they were originally created in spite of their sin. Thus the secondary cause of human free will is preserved and honored by God as a part of normal human activity. God does not override human freedom but rather works concurrently through that freedom to accomplish his purposes.

Sometimes humans make bad choices and fall into sin. But because human freedom is essential to all personal relationships, God concurs with their freedom even though he does not approve of

---

3. Oden, *The Living God*, 279, 281, 288; Grudem, *Systematic Theology*, 316–17; Wesley, *BE Works*, 9:213–20. For discussion of the concept of preservation in the early church see Pannenberg, *Systematic Theology*, 2:35–36.

4. Wesley, "On Providence," *BE Works*, 2:538–40.

5. The concept of concurrence is an extension of preservation, and indeed some theologians treat concurrence under the heading of preservation. See Calvin, *Institutes of the Christian Religion*, 1:223–25.

their sin.[6] Though God permits people to choose sin or evil, he does not directly cause either. He chose to create persons who might choose that which is contrary to his will.

Nevertheless, creatures are not left to themselves. God is present with his creatures even though he is not the cause of their actions.[7] Through his Word and the ministry of the Holy Spirit, God cooperates with his creatures in their actions and uses secondary causes to work within nonpersonal creation.[8]

GOVERNANCE

God's divine governance of the world is so pervasive in the affairs of individuals and nations that it is impossible to miss it in the biblical record from creation to the end times. In his providence God guides and directs every part of creation to his purposeful ends.

God foresaw the entry of sin and evil in creation and made provision for redeeming persons from it. Christ is God's response and solution to sin, and his work opens the door to understanding God's governance of all creation. The doctrine of God's providence is the central link between creation, sin, redemption, and the consummation.

Nothing in creation is beyond God's providential care, but the various parts of creation are treated according to their own properties and God's purposes for each. There is a major distinction between God's governing the impersonal (matter, plants, and animals) and the personal (human) parts of creation.[9]

God works through "natural" law to accomplish his purposes in impersonal creation. Physical laws normally govern inanimate creation. This enables the study of physics, chemistry, geology and astronomy, which depend on physical forces that are reliable and do not vary. Lifeless matter also makes possible living plants, and

---

6. Augustine, *NPNF* 1, 3:377–90; Calvin, *Institutes of the Christian Religion*, 3:22–24; Aquinas, *Summa Contra Gentiles*, 3:1, 558f.

7. Pannenberg, *Systematic Theology*, 2:48.

8. Oden, *The Living God*, 281–85; Grudem, *Systematic Theology*, 317–22.

9. Oden, *The Living God*, 286–89.

the natural laws of biology (e.g., cell division, reproduction, and photosynthesis) govern this area. Animals are sentient and mobile beings, yet they are not persons. They too are governed by laws appropriate to their being, which we study through the discipline of zoology. Thus God gives integrity to the nonpersonal aspects of creation through secondary causes.

Every person and every human group is in some way under the governing hand of God. But Scripture indicates that god respects the freedom he has given to individuals, so he manges their affairs without being directly responsible for the choices that they make. How is this possible?

In order to understand this, we need to take a fresh approach—a Trinitarian approach— to the way God governs human persons.[10]

JESUS AS THE MODEL: THE WAY OF UNDERSTANDING PROVIDENCE

FROM THE DIVINE PERSPECTIVE

Jesus is our model for understanding the way providence works. As God, he provides the divine perspective, and as a man, he provides a human perspective on how providence works. Both perspectives are important for understanding God's governance of creation.[11]

THE TRINITY, PERSONHOOD, AND ROLES OF GOD

With the doctrine of the Trinity, we have seen that the Bible presents God as a social being. The persons of the Trinity are intimately related to each other (Ontological Trinity) and work to build

---

10. Oden, *The Living God*, 286–93; Grudem, *Systematic Theology*, 327–32; Pope, *Compendium of Christian Theology*, 1:445ff; Pannenberg, *Systematic Theology,* 2:54–59.

11. For Jesus as a way into a Trinitarian view of providence, see T. F. Torrance, *The Christian Doctrine of God*, 221–22.

relationships with others (Economic Trinity). Thus our discussion of governance must be wrapped in relational categories.

A proper discussion of providence does not begin with God's power but his relationality. The triune God does not begin with the exercise of omnipotence over his creatures. Rather, he begins by developing relationships with human persons.

Also, human beings find their fulfillment under the governance of God. They are designed for two kinds of relationship: with the triune God and with other humans. God desires for the good of creation that human persons freely bring themselves under his loving governance.

The focus of providence is personal; God is the divine parent who cares for his children. Thus governance is not so much a matter of control, fiat, power, and authority as it is one of communication, self-giving, love, respect, and trust. Of course, authority is exercised within these parameters. When God's roles of Personal Revealer and Father are taken seriously, the whole discussion of God's governance is radically altered. In fact, it calls into question whether *governance* is the proper term. It may be that *guidance* and *direction* are more suitable terms for relationships with human persons.

PROVIDENCE: MOVING FROM GOD AS SOVEREIGN KING TO GOD AS TRIUNE BEING

Most treatments of providence generally begin with the role of God as sovereign King, how he operates with power and authority to accomplish his purposes for citizens who are under his kingly rule. The language of kingship and the role of a monarch has traditionally been the starting place for discussing his providential governance of creation.[12]

What is being proposed here is a shift in focus from God's role as sovereign King to God as the triune Being, a change from one of the metaphorical roles to the metaphysical reality of God. The

---

12. e.g., Frame, *The Doctrine of God*, 276.

role of God as sovereign King needs to be understood in light of the larger biblical perspective of God as triune Being. Before God was a King, he was a Father within a triune Being. Given a triune starting point, the priority of God's role as Father is not difficult to establish. A growing conviction among conservative theologians supports the view that the fatherhood of God must be taken more seriously in our discussions of how God relates to his creation.[13]

This shift from the sovereign King to God as Father sets God's omnipotence, sovereignty, and authority in an entirely different context, that of a loving Father who cares for and guides the growth of his children. So God's personal attributes take precedence over his relative attributes. God still has power and authority, but these now service the Father's loving heart.

The Trinitarian perspective makes it easier to understand the biblical narratives about personal as well as historical providence. God as Father is not only concerned with nations, peoples, and his overarching purposes for the world but also intimately concerned with individual men and women. So the Bible includes multiple stories about God's relationships with individuals and how he coordinated the circumstances of their lives to accomplish his purposes (e.g., Joseph and Esther).

JESUS AND THE TRINITY AS CREATOR: A TRIUNE FATHER REVEALS HIS PURPOSES FOR CREATION

Understanding God's purposes for the world is essential to his providential work in and through creation. His purposes are the ends for which he is working through his providential oversight of the world.

---

13. See the scholarly work by Feinberg, *No One Like Him*. Feinberg's extensive study on the doctrine of God does not treat the doctrine of the Trinity until chapter 10 and in the process the Trinitarian understanding of God seems to make almost no difference in the rest of the discussion of who God is or the way he relates to his creation. The primary focus is upon God in his role as sovereign King. Equally John Frame, *The Doctrine of God*, treats the Trinity last (see Chapters 27–29).

God's caring concern for creation is legitimate in itself. He models stewardship of the created order in that he takes responsibility it. Being made in God's image, Adam and Eve were given dominion over and responsibility for God's good creation (Gen. 1:26–28).

The created order is made for man and woman, for their sustenance, delight, enjoyment, use. They are to care for creation, not exploit, destroy, mismanage, or waste it. Man and woman are stewards of the impersonal creation.

The purposes of God for personal creation are distinct from those for the impersonal creation. In Scripture, God has six purpose for human persons.[14] Primarily, he desires that they share life and love out of a close personal relationship with himself. The other five flow from this desire: first, that men and women might be a living reflection of his own character; second, that they develop godly thinking; third, that they have close personal relationships; fourth, that they serve others; and finally, that they delight in and enjoy his good creation. In spite of the entrance of sin into the world (Gen. 3), it is clear that God's purposes for men and women have not changed. The realization of these purposes for them is accomplished through God's providence.

THE DISTINCTION BETWEEN GOD'S MEANS AND GOD'S PURPOSES

When providence centers on God's role as sovereign King, there is a temptation to equate God's means with his purposes. The Trinitarian understanding of God as Father reveals the distinction between purpose and means. While the Father purposes (desires) good for his children, he limits the use of his power (means) to actualize it because of he is unwilling to override their freedom of choice.

From the Trinitarian perspective, God's chief purpose is that all persons live out of a close relationship with himself. The Trinity, whose divine persons share the closest and most intimate relations,

---

14. For a more extensive discussion of God's purposes for creation, see Coppedge, *The God Who Is Triune,* Chapter 11.

made human persons in his own image so they too might share life in person-to-person relationships. God, who is love, shares love and desires to be loved in return. T. F. Torrance says that the triune God does "all in fulfillment of the purpose of his measureless Love not to exist for himself alone but to bring other beings into coexistence with himself that he may share with them his Triune fellowship of love."[15]

God's chief object, then, in light of his chief purpose, is to enable all persons to choose a shared life with himself. So the Father, who respects the freedom of his children, does not force his purposes on them but invites them into a relationship of love, and this is possible because they are providentially designed to make such a choice and thereby experience his chief purpose in life. Love, to be genuine, must be freely chosen.

This Trinitarian and familial language helps us understand why God's *plan*—to enable all persons to choose what he desires for them—is accomplished, while his *chief purpose*—that they lovingly relate to him—is not accomplished with all.

God's secondary purposes for people are evident in the creation narrative and illustrated again in the life of Jesus. But they are dependent upon God's chief purpose being carried out. Until a person shares a relationship of love with God (beginning with saving grace), it is not possible for God to accomplish his other purposes in that particular person's life.

All six purposes are best understood in terms of God as Father rather than God as sovereign King. Though the Father desires the best for his children, he does not force his purposes on them.

JESUS, THE TRINITY, AND THE ROLE OF THE KING

While God's primary roles are that of Personal Revealer and Father, he still works in creation as the sovereign King. God certainly governs Old Testament Israel as a ruler. Further, at the con-

---

15. T. F. Torrance, *The Christian Doctrine of God*, 221.

summation of history, God again will serve in the role as King, exercising the final word in sovereign authority over his creation. Scripture provides many example where God's governing rule over the nations in general and Israel in particular is illustrated (e.g., Isa. 6; Rev. 4).

Jesus appeared at a time when many Israelites expected the arrival of a Messiah, a Davidic ruler anointed by God. While Jesus uses much of this terminology to initially identify himself, he radically transformed it by modeling a different view of sovereignty and kingship. He did so by identifying his own relationship with God as primarily that of a Son to a Father. God is sovereign, but Jesus set before his disciples a Trinitarian sovereignty. The role of Father is so central to Jesus' that the disciples and the early church used "Father" as the primary way to refer to God. Sovereign kingship, therefore, was seen against the backdrop of God as Father.

This reframing counters the temptation to think of sovereignty in terms of transcendence. God as Father is separate and distinct from his people, but like a father he interacts with them as well and is personally involved in their daily lives. So God's immanence and his transcendence are kept in balance.

This means that any connection between the sovereign King and providence has to take into account the relationship of the divine persons of the Trinity. The model of sovereignty is no longer the emperor of Rome, the governor of Judea, or the king of Galilee, but the interactive communication, self-giving, care, love, and right relationships between Jesus, the Father, and the Spirit. Trinitarian sovereignty is not about omnipotence but self-giving, holy, loving relationships.

PROVIDENCE AND THE TRIUNE GOD'S PURPOSES

The triune God works in the world to accomplish his primary purpose by enabling, by grace, all person to choose a shared life of close relationship with himself (redemption). This may be referred to as a *special or personal providence* that makes it possible for individuals to choose fellowship with God and all of its benefits. This relationship begins with the initial experience of salvation by faith through Christ, continues in growth as his disciple, moves on to deeper levels in full sanctification and a life full of the Spirit, and goes on to greater stages of development in spiritual maturity. Through God's agents, personal providence arranges the circumstances of life in order for redeemed persons to continue to choose growth in their relationship of love with God.

THE TRIUNE GOD'S PERSONAL AGENTS IN PROVIDENCE

Each member of the Economic Trinity has special functions in relationship to the created order. The Father, for example, indicates the purposes of the Godhead and is most closely identified with the means God uses to make those possible. But the Son and the Spirit are God's chief agents for interacting with creation and in providentially accomplishing his purposes.

The Son of God, through the incarnation and life of Jesus, models the triune life of God and the six purposes of God for people. He demonstrates fellowship with God, he illustrates godly character, he reveals how to think as God thinks, he models close human relationships, he serves God in ministry to others, and he delights in life. The atoning work of God in Christ releases God's grace to persons so that they are enabled to receive what God desires to do in and through them.

The Spirit also plays two roles in the Economic Trinity. First, he *orders the circumstances* of life so that God's purposes can be accomplished. He coordinates the affairs of nations and more specifically the personal lives of individuals so they are in the place to make appropriate choices and receive God's best for them. Second, the Spirit *applies God's provisions*—God's grace—to individuals so they can freely choose to respond to God, and God can accomplish his work in them and fulfill his purposes. The Spirit consummates or actualizes the work of Christ.

A biblical understanding of providence includes all persons of the Economic Trinity. The Father is connected with God's purposes in creation. The Son models God's purposes and makes provision for their accomplishment through grace. The Spirit orders the circumstances for God to work in people's lives and applies the grace to individual persons so they might appropriate God's gifts.

THE TRIUNE GOD'S PROVIDENTIAL MEANS

God's grace and providence go hand in hand. Grace has two components. First, it is the unmerited favor of God toward persons; thus it is a relational term. Through grace we receive something that is not due to any merit or work on our part. Rather, it comes as a gift of God. Grace is the self-giving of God in which all of the favor of his personal presence works in relationship to us.

Second, grace is the holiness of God as enabling power. In his omnipotence God creates and preserves the universe. But when power is wrapped in the personal categories of the triune God (i.e., holiness), it is described as grace. From this perspective grace is God's enabling of persons to make choices that allow him to accomplish his purposes in their lives.

Grace is provided through the Son and is actualized by the Spirit when he enables individuals to choose God's purposes. Notice that grace is not *a thing*; it is not something people possess. Rather, it is a relational reality with the holy, triune God. When we are in fellowship with God through the Spirit, God's enabling power works through this relationship to empower us to do what he longs for. This enabling power, which comes from our relationship with God, is grace.

God's grace enables even the fallen human will to function with relative freedom. *Prevenient grace* is the grace with which God works with persons before salvation. The Spirit providentially orders life's circumstances so nonbelievers have the opportunity to respond to the invitation to fellowship with the triune God. In the book of Acts, for example, people at Antioch of Pisidia, who had not yet believed, heard the gospel proclaimed in the synagogue (Acts 13:16–43). After the initial proclamation of the gospel, but before anyone has responded in faith (Acts 13:48), God in his prevenient grace had already been at work in their midst, so Paul and Barnabas "spoke to them and urged them to continue in the grace of God" (Acts 13:43). The same grace had been at work when Apollos crossed to Achaia and on his arrival was able to greatly help "those who by grace had believed" (Acts 18:27). Grace—*prevenient grace*—had already been operative to bring them to belief. These illustrations make it clear that in spite of the drastic impact of sin, a person's will has enough freedom restored to it by grace to respond to God's revelation in faith. After the initial response of faith, grace does not cease. Rather, it is enlarged with saving grace and growing grace as the person's relationship with the triune God more fully enables him or her to respond even further to God's desires.

Providence includes the key components of God's *purposes*, his *agents* in the universe and his *means* to accomplish his ends. The implication is that for the triune God to relate person-to-person to human individuals, he must do so with respect for the freedom that is a part of their personhood. So *how* God works in the world to accomplish his purposes is in concert with his previous choice to provide persons with freedom of the will. Without this component, God would treat persons in the same category as impersonal creation, but when he relates with this component of personal freedom, humans cannot be treated as impersonal creation and retain their personhood.

JESUS' MODEL OF PROVIDENCE
FROM THE HUMAN PERSPECTIVE

Theologically Jesus serves a valuable role in helping us understand the nature of human persons and thus our anthropology. As the God-Man, his unique person, which brings into right relationship divinity and humanity, is the key to connecting a supranatural, transcendent creator God with the immanent, personal God that comes into the world and interacts with those he has made. As the theandric person, he models both Godhood and humanity.

In addition to leading us to an understanding of God's triune activity, Jesus also carries the responsibility of showing us how this providential activity works from a human perspective. By becoming fully human and taking on all of the limitations of humanity living within a fallen world, Jesus models how persons made in the image of God live under the providential direction of this triune Godhead.

JESUS: THE MODEL OF HISTORICAL PROVIDENCE

Jesus is the key to the understanding God's providential work in history. After Adam and Eve's fall into sin (Gen. 3), God initially does not work with a specific group of people (Gen. 4–11), but beginning with Abraham (Gen. 12–35) God primarily works through one nation. The plan of God for people comes to fruition in the person of Jesus, who models what God desires for the whole nation.[16]

The New Testament opens with the genealogy of Jesus, tracing his lineage from Abraham through David to the birth of Christ.[17] This shorthand history is a declaration that God has been working throughout history to accomplish his purposes through Jesus.

In Acts, Paul's overview of historical providence includes God's choice of the Patriarchs, their sojourn in Egypt, the Exodus, the wilderness wandering, the conquest of Canaan, the leadership of the judges and Samuel, the establishment of the monarchy under Saul and David, and the ministry of John the Baptist as the last forerun-

---

16. Wright, *Jesus and the Victory of God*, 147–97; *The Challenge of Jesus*, 34–53.

17. Luke's genealogy does not begin with Abraham but with Adam (Luke 3:23–28).

ner of Jesus. Jesus is the fulfillment of God's purposes throughout this significant history (Acts 13:16–31).[18]

Paul not only sees God's providential plan for Jesus extending back through history but also through the future and to the end of the age. The work of Jesus, culminating in his death and resurrection, plus the Spirit's work at Pentecost extends God's work in Israel to all peoples, both Jews and Gentiles. Paul illustrated how this works on his missionary journeys to the Gentiles (Acts 13–28). The gospel of Jesus Christ changed lives and in a matter of a few hundred years changed the whole world. So the Old Testament illustrates how historical providence worked to prepare for Jesus' coming. The Gospels present his incarnation, life, death, and resurrection, and the rest of the New Testament illustrates how Jesus changes lives, touching all of the nations of the world. So the whole sweep of history centers on the person of Jesus. This is God's historical providence.

JESUS: THE MODEL OF PERSONAL PROVIDENCE

While the metanarrative of Scripture is a testimony to general providence, it is also a testimony to God's personal or specific providence for individuals. Coordinated with the great historical events in the life of God's people are illustrations of God's personal relationships with individuals. At every major turning point in biblical history, God has at least one person who models proper human and divine relationships. But Jesus is the center of the narrative and thus the primary illustration of God's personal providence.

Jesus, fully human, illustrates in principle God's desire to relate to every person. His historical circumstances are unique, but how to relate personally to God and how to allow God to providentially work in one's life are universal principles. Jesus is born at a specific time in history, with specific parents, at a specific location, speaking a specific language, with certain distinctive physical and personality

---

18. Other sermons in the book of Acts also trace God's purposes through Israel to Jesus (see Acts 7:2–53).

HOLY LOVE: A WESLEYAN SYSTEMATIC THEOLOGY

features. His experiences are uniquely ordered by God's personal providence, and he is allowed to live out his life and complete his ministry in time and circumstances and in relationships that are all part of God's personal ordering, including his birth and resurrection.[19]

GOD'S PROVIDENTIAL ORDERING OF CIRCUMSTANCES FOR INDIVIDUALS

Jesus, the God-Man, reorders all of our thinking about providence. When he taught his disciples about God's providence Jesus started with familiar terms and concepts, but then he shifted to new and less familiar language.

The Old Testament makes large use of royal language when speaking of God's providential work. God governs the created order as sovereign King. Jesus used much of this language to discuss the kingdom of God and his messianic role within it. But once he identified himself as the long-expected Messiah in the line of David, he filled these terms with new meaning. When speaking of God, Jesus introduced family language, speaking of God primarily as his Father. This introduces what will become Trinitarian language about how they are to know him and how he relates to the world. All but three New Testament epistles begin with a reference to God as Father, but not a single letter begins with a reference to God as King, Creator, or Judge. Clearly, Jesus' relationship to his Father changed the way his followers relate to God and changed their perspective of how God relates to the world.

This shift to family language requires a corresponding shift in the ordering of the roles of God and the attributes of God. When royal language is dominant, the relative attributes (omnipotence, omniscience, omnipresence, wisdom) are seen as primary. The temptation is to view God as an absolute dictator who can arbitrarily choose

---

19. On personal as well as historical providence, see Wesley, "On Providence," *BE Works*, 2:548; "An Estimate of the Manners of the Present Times," *Works*, 11:160.

whatever he wants without consideration of others. The focus is on power and authority; the King always gets what he wants.

The fact that God has multiple other roles (e.g., Redeemer, Shepherd, Teacher, and Friend) modifies this portrait of God as a despot or dictator. Scripture presents the multiple roles of God for this very reason. No one role becomes absolute, each being modified by the others.[20] When Jesus introduced God as Father, this changed his disciples' perspective on God's sovereignty. The emphasis shifted from God's relative attributes to his personal (sociality, life, reason, imagination, emotions, will, freedom, responsibility, creativity) and moral attributes (holiness and love expressed in righteousness, truth, purity, grace, and goodness). Thus the disciples' relationship with God did not begin with his omnipotence but with his personal attributes and the corresponding moral attributes.

Christian theology, based on Jesus' teaching and salvific work, must take into account all of the attributes of God, and all of God's attributes are pertinent to the doctrine of providence. However, from a Trinitarian perspective, which begins with God as Father, the relative attributes (e.g., omnipotence) are subordinate to the personal attributes (e.g., freedom) and moral attributes (e.g., love, righteousness, goodness). The coming of the Son of the Father has irrevocably altered our view of God and his providence.

God's Providential Ways

Through his providence, God has a *plan* for individual lives. Here we find a tension between God's desire for the absolute best and the reality of human choices, which may limit the appropriation of God's desire. Because our Trinitarian perspective does not permit an arbitrary decision on God's part to make choices for us, he may have to modify his plans for individual lives, but he does so in light of his foreknowledge of our choices. The Father knows the choices of his children without causing them. But through the

---

20. On the variety of roles that give a spectrum form distance to intimacy, see Coppedge, *Portraits of God*, 394–95.

agency of his Son and his Spirit he uses means (grace) to order life's circumstances for individuals in light of their free choices.[21]

Great wisdom is required to accomplish God's plan for individuals in light of their choices. If they freely choose his will, their lives more closely match his ideal plan. If they choose not to follow his perfect will, there are fewer blessings and goods that God can effectively accomplish in their lives.

Jesus Illustrates the Work of Providence

God's relationship to Jesus as a man is an indicator of how he desires to relate to other men and women. One key example of this comes in the garden of Gethsemane. On this last evening of Jesus' life, God in his providence had coordinated all the circumstances of his life, including the free choices of those around him. So God's providence includes wrong choices: the sinful choices of the Jewish leadership, the Roman governor, and a disciple. But God was able to coordinate even the sinful choices of Caiaphas, Pilate, and Judas to accomplish his specific plan for Jesus. Without overriding their freedom, God used their choices to bring his plan for Jesus' to fruition.

In his garden prayer, Jesus models the appropriate human response, using the most intimate form of address to God— "Abba, Father"—in his request that this cup be removed from him (Mark 14:36). So this petition is not primarily to the sovereign God but to his Father, with the full acknowledgement that the Father may have a plan Jesus does not fully understand. He approaches God's providential role in trust and thereby demonstrates total obedience to the whole will of God. "Not what I will, but what thou wilt." This response of trust and obedience makes it possible for God to accomplish his full and best purposes for him.

---

21. For more on foreknowledge and freedom, see Feinberg, *No One Like Him*, 735–75, and Beilby and Eddy, *Divine Foreknowledge*.

The value of using Jesus as an example is that it removes the temptation to always consider God's providence in terms of blessing, prosperity, health, and lack of pain. For Jesus, the cost is high; pain and death were part of God's plan for him. Apparently, the providential working of God as Father does not exempt his children from all difficult circumstances. If Jesus had sought God primarily as sovereign King, he could have called for twelve legions of angels to deliver him from his circumstances (Matt. 26:53). But he relates to God as Father and therefore completely trusts his fatherly providence.

Ordering Circumstances

How does God order the circumstances of life around the personal freedom of individuals? We know his plans include his purposes, he limits himself by human freedom, and he uses his means. But more specifically he orders circumstances through permission, restraint, overruling, prevention, and guidance.

1. As Father, God limits his own choices by *permitting* persons to make free choices. He desires this freedom to be properly used to seek him and therefore get his best, but he permits poor and even sinful choices that lead to suffering. Genuine freedom can be misused. As a Father, God permits people to choose sin and evil, even though he does not approve of those choices. We must live with our choices, and the drastic consequences of wrong choices are part of his providential education.

2. The Father also works in the lives of individuals by *hindrance*. Though he does not coerce humans, he may put obstacles in their way when they are hurting themselves or others. Human parents often protect their children by limiting the toys they can play with by fencing them in.[22]

---

22. Of course, in spite of their best efforts, a child may still find a way to do harm.

This hindering does not override the freedom of individuals, but it may coordinate the free choices of many people as well as some parts of the impersonal creation to hinder a person from certain harmful consequences to himself or others (Gen. 20:6).

3. God may sometimes *overrule* the consequences of choices, especially when they are drastically negative. This is not an overruling of free and rational choices but involves such things as lapse of memory, confusion, distractions, and alternative thoughts coming to mind. God sometimes overrules to keep sinners from harming themselves and others and indirectly nudges them toward decisions beyond their own understanding. Sometimes God overrules the consequences of wrong choices. The story of Jacob's sons selling Joseph into slavery is an example. God certainly did not approve of the wrong choices and the threat of murder. So he overrode the consequences of their decision in order to get Joseph to a place where he could fulfill God's plan to save the Hebrews and bless Egypt (Gen. 50:20). So God is regularly working through circumstances, relationships, events, and impersonal creation to override or prevent some of the drastic implications of evil in some circumstances.

4. God also *prevents* temptation from becoming overpoweringly and having its full way. As 1 John states, "Greater is he that is in you than the one who is in you is greater than the one who is in the world" (1 John 4:4). Because of this, God can externally open ways of escape or internally provide grace to resist temptation (1 Cor. 10:13).[23] He often coordinates the free choices of others and external circumstances of impersonal creation to prevent individuals from being unduly harmed or missing God's way.

---

23. Oden, *The Living God*, 300–2.

5. God also *guides* people. The Spirit of God, working through prevenient grace, arranges the circumstances of Christians, and to some degree even non-Christians, so that they are guided to make appropriate decisions. The Spirit coordinates activities, events, natural laws, secondary causes,and so forth to optimize the opportunities people have to choose what God wants for their lives.

To arrange certain circumstances in an individual's life, God's guidance does not necessarily require that the individual chooses correctly. But many times (if not most) this is the case. The more godly decisions a person makes, the greater the probability of getting God's best in his life.

The means of guidance God has at his disposal are legion. The most significant for Christians, and sometimes even nonbelievers, is his Word. Guidance also comes through other persons, impressions on the mind, imagination, emotions, events, circumstances, interruptions, changes, and even distractions. It may come through finances, reading books, or the media. Sometimes God's guidance comes through sickness, accidents, tragedy, or death. These and other circumstances of our lives may be part of God's providential guidance. Sometimes God uses these and other tools in a providential way relative to timing. While God does not override human choices, he may delay, hinder, prevent, or override the consequences of certain poor choices.

God uses these tools of providence through his relative attributes. He is able to work in our lives because of his omnipresence and omniscience. By using his self-limited omnipotence and wisdom, he is able to coordinate all of the circumstances of life. As Wesley said, "The whole frame of divine providence is so constituted as to afford man every possible help, in order to his doing good and eschewing evil, which can be done without turning man in to a machine; without making him incapable of virtue or vice, reward or punishment."[24]

In summary, the Trinitarian perspective on providence is primarily shaped by Jesus' relationship to God as his loving Father. Thus in his providential work in persons, God does not force decisions but respects their freedom to choose. Nevertheless, he works through the circumstances of their lives to give them the opportunity to fellowship with him. God the Spirit, working through the prevenient grace that has been provided by God the Son, orders circumstances through various means so that God can enable person to freely choose his design for their lives. If this freedom is used appropriately, the Father's purposes and best plans will be actualized.[25]

---

24. Wesley, "On Providence," *BE Works*, 2:541.
25. Pope, *Compendium of Christian Theology,* 1:440–44.

Bibliography

Alden, Richard. *"aheb." TWOT* 1:14–15.

Aquinas, Thomas. *Summa Contra Gentiles.* 5 vols. Notre Dame: University of Notre Dame Press, 1955–57.

_____. *Summa Theologica.* AD 1265–73. Edited by Thomas Gilby. 18 vols. Reprint, Garden City, NY: Image, 1969.

Aulén, Gustaf. *The Faith of the Christian Church.* Translated by Eric H. Wahlstrom. Philadelphia: Muhlenberg, 1960.

Barnes, Michael. "Augustine in Contemporary Trinitarian Theology." In *Theological Studies.* Vol. 56 (June 1995).

Barth, Karl. *Church Dogmatics* 3/3. Edited by G. W. Bromiley and T. F. Torrance. Translated by G. T. Thompson and Harold Knight. Edinburgh: T & T Clark, 1958.

Baukham, Richard. *God Crucified: Monotheism and Christology in the New Testament.* Grand Rapids: Eerdmans, 1999.

Beckwith, C. A. "Holiness of God," *NSRE* 5:316–19.

Begbie, Jeremy. "Through Music: Sound, Mix." In *Beholding the Glory: Incarnation through the Arts*, edited by Jeremy Begbie. Grand Rapids: Baker, 2000.

Beilby, James K. and Paul R. Eddy, eds. *Divine Foreknowledge: Four Views.* Downers Grove: Intervarsity, 2001.

Bobrinskoy, Boris. *The Mystery of the Trinity.* Crestwood, NY: St. Vladimir's Seminary Press, 1999.

Boyd, Gregory A. "The Open Theism View." In *Divine Foreknowledge*. Edited by James K. Beilby and Paul R. Eddy. Downers Grove: InterVarsity, 2001.

Brunner, Emil. *The Christian Doctrine of Creation and Redemption*. Translated by Olive Wyon. Philadelphia: Westminster, 1952.

_____. *The Christian Doctrine of God*. Translated by Olive Wyon. London: Lutterworth Press, 1949.

Caird, G. B. *The Language and Imagery of the Bible*. Grand Rapids: Eerdmans, 1997.

Calvin, John. *Institutes of the Christian Religion*. 4 vols. Translated by John Allen. Philadelphia: Presbyterian Board, 1813.

Coffey, David. *Deus Trinitas: The Doctrine of the Triune God*. Oxford: Oxford University Press, 1999.

Coleman, Robert E. *The Master Plan of Evangelism*. Old Tappan: Flynn Revell, 1973.

Coppedge, Allan. *Biblical Principles of Discipleship*. Grand Rapids: Zondervan, 1986.

_____. *The God Who Is Triune*. Downers Grove, IL: InterVarsity, 2007.

_____. *Holy Living: Godliness in the Old Testament*. Wilmore: The Barnabas Foundation, 2000.

_____. *Portraits of God*. Downers Grove, IL: InterVarsity, 2001.

Del Colle, Ralph. "The Triune God." In *The Cambridge Companion to Christian Doctrine*. Edited by Colin Gunton. Cambridge: Cambridge University Press, 1997.

DeMargerie, Bertrand. *Christian Trinity and History*. Petersham: St. Bede's Publications, 1982.

Dupré, Louis. *The Common Life: the Origins of Trinitarian Mysticism and Its Development by Jan Ruusbroec*. New York: Crossroad, 1984.

Eichrodt, Walther. *Theology of the Old Testament*. Translated by J. A. Baker. 6th ed. 2 vols. Philadelphia: Westminster, 1961.

Feinberg, John. *No One Like Him*. Wheaton: Crossway Books, 2001.

Forsyth, P. T. *The Cruciality of the Cross*. Wake Forest: Chanticlear, 1983.

Fortman, Edmund J. *The Triune God*. Grand Rapids: Baker, 1972.

Frame, John M. *The Doctrine of God*. Phillipsburg, NJ: P & R, 2002.

Ganssle, Gregory E., ed. *God and Time: Four Views*. Downers Grove, IL: InterVarsity, 2001.

Glueck, Nelson. Hesed *in the Bible*. Cincinnati: Hebrew Union College Press, 1967.

Greene, Garrett. *Imagining God*. San Francisco: Harper & Row, 1989.

Grenz, Stanley J. *Rediscovering the Triune God: The Trinity in Contemporary Theology*. Minneapolis: Fortress Press, 2004.

Grudem, Wayne. *Systematic Theology*. Grand Rapids: Zondervan, 1994.

Gruenler, Royce Gorden. *The Trinity in the Gospel of John*. Eugene: Wipf & Stock, 1986.

Gunton, Colin, ed. *The Cambridge Companion to Christian Doctrine*. Cambridge: Cambridge University Press, 1997.

_____. *The Promise of Trinitarian Theology*. Edinburgh: T & T Clark, 1991.

Guthrie, Donald. *New Testament Theology*. Downers Grove, IL: InterVarsity, 1981.

Harrelson, Walter. "The Idea of Agape in the New Testament." *The Journal of Religion* 31:3 (July 1951): 169–82.

Harris, R. Laird. *"hesed." TWOT* 1:305–07.

Harrison, E. F. "Holiness." *ISBE* 2:724–28.

Hart, David Bentley. *The Beauty of the Infinite*. Grand Rapids: Eerdmans, 2003.

Hill, William J. *The Three-Personned God*. Washington: Catholic University of America Press, 1982.

Houston, James M. "Spirituality and the Doctrine of the Trinity." In *Christ in Our Place*. Edited by Trevor Hard and Daniel Thimell. Exeter: PaterNoster Press, 1989.

Jacob, Edmond. *Theology of the Old Testament*. New York: Harper, 1958.

Jenson, Robert. *Systematic Theology, Vol. 1: The Triune God*. Oxford: Oxford University Press, 1997.

_____. *Triune Identity*. Philadelphia: Fortress Press, 1982.

Kasper, Walter. *The God of Jesus Christ*. Translated by Matthew J. O'Connell. New York: Crossroad, 1999.

Kaufmann, Yehezkel. *The Religion of Israel*. Chicago: University of Chicago Press, 1960.

Kay, J. W. "Man's Love for God in Deuteronomy and the Father/Teacher-Son/Pupil Relationship." *Vetus Testamentum* 22:4 (Oct 1972): 426–35.

Kelly, J. N. D. *Early Christian Creeds*. New York: D. McKay, 1960.

Kittel, Rudolf. *NSRE* 5:317.

Knight, George A. F. *A Christian Theology of the Old Testament*. Richmond: John Knox, 1959.

La Cugna, Catherine. *God or Us*. San Francisco: Harper, 1991.

Leitch, A. H. *ZPBD* 5:105.

Lewis, G. R. "Attributes of God." *EDT* 456.

Lonergan, Bernard J. F. *The Way to Nicea*. Philadelphia: Westminster Press, 1976.

Lossky, Vladimir. *The Mystical Theology of the Eastern Church*. Crestwood: St. Vladimir's Press, 1998.

Mascall, E. L. *Existence and Analogy*. London: Longmans, Green and Company, 1949.

McCarthy, Dennis J. "Notes on the Love of God in Deuteronomy and the Father-Son Relationship between Yahweh and Israel." *Catholic Biblical Quarterly* 27:2 (1965): 144–47.

McComisky, Thomas. "*qadosh.*" *TWOT* 2:786–89.

de Molina, Luis. *On Divine Foreknowledge: Part IV of the Concordia.* Translated by Alfred J. Freddoso. Ithica: Cornell University Press, 1988.

Moltmann, Jürgen. *The Trinity in the Kingdom.* Minneapolis: Fortress, 1993.

Moody, Dale. *The Word of Truth: A Summary of Christian Doctrine Based on Biblical Revelation.* Grand Rapids: Eerdmans, 1981.

Morris, Leon. *The Testaments of Love.* Grand Rapids: Eerdmans, 1981.

Muilenburg, James. "Holiness," *IDB* 2:616–25.

Nygren, Anders. *Agape and Eros.* Philadelphia: Westminster, 1953.

Oden, Thomas C. *The Living God.* San Francisco: Harper & Row, 1987.

Oehler, Gustoff. *Theology of the Old Testament.* New York: Funk & Wagnall, 1883.

Oswalt, John N. "The God of Abraham, Isaac and Jacob: The Trinity in the Old Testament." In *The Trinity: An Essential for Faith in Our Time.* Edited by Andrew Stirling. Nappanee: Evangel Press, 2002.

Otto, Rudolph. *The Idea of the Holy.* London: Oxford University Press, 1928.

Outka, Gene H. *Agape: An Ethical Analysis.* New Haven: Yale University Press, 1972.

Packer, J. I. "Good." *NBD* 433–34.

Pannenberg, Wolfhart. *Systematic Theology.* 3 vols. Translated by Geoffrey W. Bromiley. Grand Rapids: Eerdmans, 1991–97.

Paul, Ian. "Metaphor." *Dictionary for Theological Interpretation for the Bible*. Edited by Kevin J VanHoozer. Grand Rapids: Baker, 2005.

Pelikan, Jaroslav. *The Emergence of the Catholic Tradition*. Chicago: University of Chicago Press, 1971.

Pinnock, Clark H. *Most Moved Mover*. Grand Rapids: Baker, 2001.

Pope, William Burt. *A Compendium of Christian Theology*. 3 vols. London: Wesleyan-Methodist Book Room, 1880.

Prestige, G. L. *God in Patristic Thought*. London: SPCK, 1952.

Procksch, Otto. "ἅγιος." *TDNT* 1:88–97, 100–12.

Quell, Gottfried. "αγάπη." *TDNT* 1:21–35.

Rahner, Karl. *The Trinity*. Translated by Joseph Donceel. New York: Crossroad, 1997.

de Regnon, Theodore. *Etudes de Theologie Positive sur la Sainte Trinite*. 2 vols. Paris, 1892.

Richard of St. Victor, *The Twelve Patriarchs; The Mystical Ark; Book Three of the Trinity*. Translated by Grover A. Zinn. New York: Paulist Press, 1979.

Richards, Jay Wesley. *The Untamed God: A Philosophical Exploration of Divine Perfection, Simplicity and Immutability*. Downers Grove, IL: InterVarsity, 2003.

Roy, Steve. *How Much Does God Foreknow? A Comprehensive Biblical Study*. InterVarsity, 2006.

Ruysbroeck, J. *The Spiritual Espousals and Other Works*. Edited by J. A. Wiseman. New York, 1985.

Sakenfeld, Katharine D. *The Meaning of* Hesed *in the Hebrew Bible: A New Inquiry*. Missoula, MT: Scholars Press, 1978.

Sherry, Patrick J. "Analogy Reviewed" and "Analogy Today." *Philosophy* 51 (1976): 337–45, 431–46.

Snaith, Norman H. *Distinctive Ideas of the Old Testament*. New York: Schocken, 1964.

Spicq, Ceslas. *Agape in New Testament*. 3 vols. St. Louis: B Herder, 1963–66.

Stählin, Gustov. "φιλέω." *TDNT* 9:113–71.

Toon, Peter. "Lovingkindness," *EDT* 661–62.

_____. *Our Triune God: A Biblical Portrait of the Trinity*. Wheaton, IL: Victor Books, 1996.

Torrance, J. B. "Contemplating the Trinitarian Mystery of Christ." In *Alive to God*, edited by J. I. Packer and L. Wilkinson. Downers Grove: InterVarsity Press, 1992.

Torrance, Thomas F. *The Christian Doctrine of God*. Edinburgh: T & T Clark, 1996.

_____. *The Trinitarian Faith: The Evangelical Theology of the Ancient Catholic Church*. Edinburgh: T & T Clark, 1988.

_____. *Trinitarian Perspectives: Toward Doctrinal Agreement*. Edinburgh: T & T Clark, 1994.

Traina, Robert A. *Methodical Bible Study*. New York: Ganis and Harris, 1952.

Vriezen, Theodorus C. *An Outline of Old Testament Theology*. Newton, MA: C. T. Bradford, 1970.

Wainwright, Arthur W. *The Trinity in the New Testament*. London" SPCK, 1962.

Wallis, Gerhard. "*aheb*." *TDOT* 1:99–118.

Warfield, B. B. "The Terminology of Love in the New Testament." *Princeton Theological Review* 16 (1918): 1–45.

Wesley, John. *The Works of John Wesley*. Thomas Jackson, ed. 14 vols. 3rd ed. 1872. Reprint, Grand Rapids: Baker, 1979.

William of St. Thierry, *The Enigma of Faith*. Edited by J. D. Anderson. Kalamazoo: 1974.

Wood, A. Skevington. "Holiness." *ZPEB* 3:173–83.

Wood, Leon. *The Spirit of God in the Old Testament*. Grand Rapids: Zondervan, 1976.

Wright, N. T. *The Challenge of Jesus*. Downers Grove, IL: InterVarsity, 1999.

_____. *Jesus and the Victory of God*. Minneapolis: Fortress, 1996.

_____. *The Resurrection of the Son of God*. Minneapolis: Fortress Press, 2003.

Zizioulas, John D. *Being as Communion*. Crestwood: St. Vladimir's Seminary Press, 1995.

Index

Scripture References

OLD TESTAMENT

Genesis
    1:1 37
    1:1–2 29
    1:26 37
    2:7 29
    3:22 37
    11:6–7 37
    16:7 33
    16:13 33
    18:1–2 35
    18:16–17 35
    21:17–19 33
    22:11–12, 15–16 33
    31:11 34
    32:24–30 34, 35
    48:15–16 34

Exodus
    2–6 34
    3:4 33
    3:5 35
    3:14 15
    4:22–23 28, 29
    14:19 34
    23:20–21 34
    23:23 34
    32–34 34
    32:34–33:14 34

Numbers
    6:24–27 36
    11:29 30
    22:31–35) 34
    24:1–2 30
    27:18 30

Deuteronomy
    4:6 37
    6:4 10, 28
    8:5 28
    32:6 28

Joshua
    5:15 35

Judges
    1:4 34
    3:9–10 30
    6:11–23 34
    6:14 34
    6:34, 36 30
    11:27–29 30
    13:3–22 34
    13:21–22 34
    13:24–25 30

1 Samuel
    3:19–21 32
    10:6–7 30
    16:12–13 30
    16:13, 18 30

2 Samuel
    7:14 29

24:16 34

2 Kings
   3:12 32

1 Chronicles
   21:27 34

2 Chronicles
   15:1–2 30
   20:13–14 30
   24:20 30

Job
   10:8–12 33
   12:13 32
   33:4 30
   104:24 33

Psalms
   2:7–8 36
   19:42 32
   68:5 28
   89:26–27 28, 29
   103:1, 13 28
   119:25 32
   119:105 32
   119:169 32

Proverbs
   1:20–23 33
   3:12 29
   3:19–20 33
   8:1–36 33
   8:22 33
   8:22–31 33
   9:1–6 33
   14:31 33
   22:2 33

Micah
   7–8 30

Isaiah
   1:2, 4 28
   6:3 36
   6:8 37
   9:1–7 27
   11:1–2 26, 27
   11:2 26, 33
   11:2–3 27
   31:2 32

32:1 26
42:1 26
42:1–4 27
48:16 31
59:21 19
61:1 31
61:1–2 17
61:1–4 26
63:16 28
64:8 28

Jeremiah
   3:19, 22 28
   10:12 33
   31:9 28

Ezekiel
   2:1–2 30
   11:15 30
   36:14 27
   36, 37, 39 26
   37:24–26 27
   37:27 27
   39:25–29 27
   40–42 35
   43:1–6 35

Daniel
   2:22–23 32
   5:14, 17–18 30

Haggai
   2:4–7 31
   2:5b–7a 31

Zechariah
   1:1–6:8 34
   1:12 34

Matthew
   1:13, 20 16
   1:18, 20 10, 17, 27
   1:20–23 20, 21
   2:15 10
   3:11 16, 27
   3:16 27
   10:18–20 18
   12:22–37 17
   12:28 17
   22:43 17

28:18–20 23
28:19 20, 21, 24
28:19–20 22
28:20 24

Mark

1:8 16, 27
1:10 27
1:10–11 21
1:24 27
3:11 17
3:28–30 17
16:19 21

Luke

1:35 10, 16, 20
3:16 16, 27
3:22 17, 27
4:1 27
4:1–14 17
4:18 17, 31
4:34 27
10:18–20 17
11:13 17, 18
11:20 17
12:11–12 17
24:47–49 19
24:49 20

John

1:1 15, 32
1:1, 14, 18 10
1:14–18 10
1:32 27
1:32–33 16
1:32–34 20
1:33 27
3:3–8 17
4:24 18
5:17 15
5:19–29 15
7:37–39 17
8:58 15
10:30 15
10:34 15
10:35, 38 15
10:38 15
14:7 15
14:9 10, 15

14:10–11 15
14:16 17, 18
14:26 17, 20
16:13 20
16:13–14 17
17:11, 21, 22 15
17:21 15
20:21–22 17, 20
20:21–23 17

Acts

1:3–5 20
1:4–5 19
2:2 29
2:33 18
7–8 20
10:38 18
11:16 27
13:33 36
28:23, 25 20

Romans

1:1–4 20
5:5 19
8:2 18
8:27 19
9:1 18
15:13 19
15:30 20

1 Corinthians

2:1–4 21
2:4–5 19
2:10–15 19
3:16 19
6:19 19
8:4 15
8:6 15
14:2 19
15:57 21

2 Corinthians

1:21–22 20
3:17–18 18
5:5 19
13:14 20

Galatians

1:3 21
3:14 18

5:5–6 18
5:22–24 18
6:7–8, 16–17 21

Ephesians
1:3 21
1:13–14 18
3:5–6 18
6:17 19
6:23 21
11:19 19
36:26–27 19
37:14 19

Philippians
1:2 21
2:5–11 15
4:19–20 21

Colossians
1:2 21
1:15–20 15
4:12 21

1 Thessalonians
1:3–5 20
4:8 19
5:18–19 20

2 Thessalonians
1:2 21
3:5 21

1 Timothy
1:2 21
6:14–15 21

2 Timothy
1:2 21
4:1 21

Titus
1:4 21
3:4–6 21

Philemon
1:3 21

Hebrews
1:1–2 21
1:1–8 15
1:5 36
13:20 21

James
1:1 21

1 Peter
1:2 21
1:11 18
5:10 21

2 Peter
1:2 21
1:16–17 15
1:21 19

1 John
1:2–3 15
1:3 21
2:22–24 15
5:20 21

2 John
3, 9 21

Jude
1, 20–21 21

Revelation
1:4–6 20
4:8 36
22:17–18 20

A

Adoptionism 42

agapē 91

'āhēb 89, 90, 110

Alexandria, Council of 44

analogy 39, 52, 65, 75, 79, 81, 82, 83, 84, 134, 135, 136, 139

angel of the Lord 33, 34, 35, 38

Antioch, Council of 43, 154

Aquinas, Thomas 50, 85, 134, 145

archē 42

Arianism 42, 44, 46, 47
Arians 16, 33, 45, 47, 49

Aristotle 135

Arius 44, 45

Athanasius 50, 51, 73, 79, 99

attributes
    absolute 74, 95, 96, 115, 116,
        123, 124, 127, 129, 130
    moral 86, 92, 93, 95, 96,
        108, 110, 111, 114, 115,
        118, 119, 122, 124, 129,
        130, 140, 158
    personal 86, 95, 96, 97, 98,
        108, 110, 114, 115, 118,
        119, 120, 124, 127, 129,
        131, 144, 148, 158
    relative 95, 96, 115, 116, 117,
        118, 122, 148, 157, 158,
        162

Augustine 50, 51, 82, 145

B

baptism 23, 24, 25
    of Jesus 16, 17, 27, 42, 43,
        66, 99
    of the Holy Spirit 19

baptismal formula 23

Barth, Karl 51, 52, 143

begotten 36, 48, 70, 71, 100, 140
    only begotten 47

Berkhof, Louis 51

Boethius 50, 103

Bridegroom. *See* role: Bridegroom

Brunner, Emil 14, 51, 88, 110, 113,
    134, 142

C

Caird, G. B. 136

Calvin, John 59, 144, 145

Cappadocian Fathers 51

chance 141, 142

Christianity 49, 54

Christology 43, 137

classical theism 115, 117, 132

coinherence 48, 55, 75, 76, 107

concurrence 143, 144

consensual 49

Constantinople, Council of 40, 46,
    54

consubstantial; consubstantiality
    54, 55, 97

Coppedge, Allan 4, 24, 29, 30, 38,
    49, 65, 89, 92, 108, 117, 123,
    134, 137, 149, 158

cosmos 138, 143

creation 15, 33, 44, 45, 48, 50, 55,
    56, 57, 58, 60, 61, 62, 64, 65,
    66, 67, 68, 74, 95, 102, 103,
    104, 106, 107, 109, 117, 118,
    119, 122, 125, 126, 127, 128,
    129, 130, 131, 132, 134, 135,
    136, 138, 141, 142, 143, 144,
    145, 146, 147, 148, 149, 150,
    151, 152, 153, 154, 161

creativity 74, 106, 107, 144, 158

Creator 38, 125, 128, 141, 142. *See
    also* role: Creator

D

deism 141, 142

Descartes, René 51

Didymus the Blind 73

Disciples 22

dualism 125

E

Ecumenical Council, Fifth 54

Eichrodt, Walther 110

emotions 74, 95, 102, 104, 105,
    106, 144, 158, 162

Enlightenment 51

eros 91

essence 20, 36, 45, 46, 47, 48, 49, 50, 54, 55, 67, 68, 70, 72, 73, 74, 75, 76, 78, 79, 86, 88, 92, 93, 100, 107, 108, 114, 124, 125, 129, 130, 139, 140

F

Faith of the Christian Church 88

fatalism 141, 142

Father 12, 13, 14, 15, 16, 17, 18, 19, 20, 21, 22, 23, 24, 27, 28, 29, 36, 38, 42, 43, 44, 45, 46, 47, 48, 49, 56, 57, 58, 59, 60, 61, 62, 63, 64, 65, 66, 67, 68, 69, 70, 71, 72, 73, 75, 76, 77, 80, 82, 83, 87, 88, 91, 97, 99, 100, 101, 102, 103, 104, 105, 106, 108, 113, 120, 123, 129, 132, 135, 136, 138, 139, 140, 147, 148, 149, 150, 151, 152, 153, 157, 158, 159, 160, 163

Feinberg, John 51, 132, 148, 159

firstborn 28

Fletcher, John 52

foreknowledge 116, 120, 121, 122, 131, 158, 159

foreordination 121

Forsyth, P. T. 88

Frame, John 51, 135, 147, 148

freedom 74, 105, 106, 107, 110, 112, 118, 121, 122, 130, 142, 144, 146, 149, 150, 153, 154, 158, 159, 160, 161, 163

Friend. *See* role: Friend

G

generalization, law of 22

glorification 17

God-Man 97, 128, 155, 157

goodness 74, 78, 89, 92, 93, 95, 105, 110, 113, 114, 144, 158

gospel 12, 17, 22, 49, 154, 156

governance 131, 143, 145, 146, 147

grace 21, 43, 61, 62, 63, 74, 78, 89, 90, 92, 93, 95, 105, 110, 112, 114, 126, 144, 150, 151, 152, 153, 154, 158, 159, 161, 162, 163. *See also* prevenient grace

Great Commission 12, 24, 103

Gregory of Nazianzus 73

Grudem, Wayne 12, 51, 142, 143, 144, 145, 146

Gruenler, Royce 68

Gunton, Colin 51, 52, 53, 103, 143

Guthrie, Donald 114

H

Harris, Murray 22, 89

Hart, David Bentley 52, 57

hesed 73, 89, 90, 110

holiness 36, 72, 73, 74, 76, 77, 81, 86, 87, 88, 89, 90, 91, 92, 93, 95, 102, 105, 107, 108, 109, 110, 111, 112, 113, 114, 115, 116, 117, 123, 124, 140, 153, 158

homoousion; homoousios 47, 48, 50, 55, 59, 67, 68, 72, 73, 74, 75, 76, 89, 97

Husband. *See* role: Husband

hypostasis, hypostases 33, 55

hypostatic union 48, 98

I

Ignatius of Antioch 43

image of God (imago Dei) 82, 97, 98, 126, 138, 155

imagination 74, 95, 102, 103, 104, 105, 108, 120, 144, 158, 162

immanence 109, 118, 125, 128, 132, 133, 151

immutability 95, 96, 115, 129, 130

impassible 104

incarnation 10, 16, 17, 19, 26, 28, 41, 43, 55, 59, 62, 66, 69, 87, 112, 116, 125, 128, 130, 131, 138, 152, 156

infinity 75, 95, 115, 124, 126, 127, 128

J

Jacob, Edmund 31, 34, 111, 161

Jenson, Robert W. 22, 30, 50, 52, 85, 99

Judaism 41

Judge 65, 113, 135, 136, 138, 139, 157

K

Kant, Immanuel 51

Kasper, Walter 16, 29, 48, 51, 52, 53, 57, 76, 77, 79, 80

Kaufmann, Yehezkel 64

King 4, 65, 77, 113, 117, 124, 132, 135, 136, 138, 139, 140, 147, 148, 149, 150, 151, 157, 158, 160

L

LaCugna, Catherine 52

Lewis, G. R. 114

Lonergan, Bernard 43, 44, 45, 51

love 19, 52, 61, 63, 73, 74, 75, 76, 77, 78, 82, 83, 86, 89, 90, 91, 92, 93, 95, 100, 101, 104, 105, 106, 107, 110, 111, 114, 115, 116, 117, 124, 127, 129, 140, 147, 149, 150, 151, 152, 158

M

marriage
at Cana 107

Mascall, E. L. 134

Messiah 10, 13, 14, 26, 27, 31, 33, 36, 65, 151, 157

metaphor 135, 136, 138

miracles 43, 142

modalism 42, 44, 46, 52
modalistic monarchianism 43–44
Sabellianism 43

Moltmann, Jürgen 51, 52, 78, 98, 100

monarchianism 42, 43, 44

monotheism 27, 28, 29, 37, 41, 42, 45, 51, 52, 64, 65, 67, 124

moral capacity 104, 105, 110

moral holiness 110

Morris, Leon 91

N

Nicea, Council of 43, 44, 45, 46

Nicene Creed 46, 47, 49, 75

O

Oden, Thomas C. 12, 20, 22, 23, 38, 39, 43, 44, 49, 51, 93, 95, 106, 116, 120, 124, 127, 130, 142, 143, 144, 145, 146, 161

omnipotent; omnipotence 74, 95, 96, 115, 116, 117, 118, 135, 144, 147, 148, 151, 153, 157, 158, 162 omnipresent; omnipresence 74, 95, 115, 116, 117, 118, 119, 127, 144, 157, 162

ontology 48, 69, 70

opera ad extra 57, 66

opera ad intra 70, 76, 140

order of being 34, 57, 96, 111, 113, 127

order of knowing 57, 96, 110, 113, 124

Otto, Rudolf 117

ousia 45, 55, 56, 72, 73, 74, 76, 86, 88, 89, 92, 93, 102, 111

P

Palamas, Gregory 51

panentheism 127

Pannenberg, Wolfhart 13, 24, 51, 52, 60, 85, 134, 143, 144, 145, 146

pantheism 127, 141, 142

particularization, law of 22

Pelikan, Jaroslav 43, 44, 45

Pentecost 10, 19, 20, 26, 41, 55, 66, 109, 111, 156

perichoresis 48, 49, 50, 55, 67, 73, 75, 76, 81, 102, 107, 125

Personal Revealer 65, 137, 138, 139, 140, 147, 150

personhood 19, 73, 85, 86, 95, 97, 98, 99, 100, 101, 102, 103, 104, 105, 107, 108, 110, 120, 124, 126, 127, 154

philosophy 73, 96, 114, 127

Physician. *See* role: Physician

Pinnock, Clark 121

plurality 10, 28, 30, 33, 34, 35, 37, 38, 65

polytheism 42, 64

Pope, W. B. 85, 114, 124, 129, 143, 146, 163

power 17, 29, 92, 115, 116, 117, 118, 119, 122, 132, 135, 144, 147, 148, 149, 153, 158

preservation 143, 144

prevenient grace 63, 144, 154, 162, 163

Priest 65, 138, 139

process theology 127

Procksch, Otto 88, 89, 90, 111

prophet 30, 109

providence 75, 122, 142, 158, 159, 160, 162, 163
doctrine of 141, 142, 143, 158
general 156
historical 148, 155, 156, 157

providential governance 147

purity 74, 78, 92, 93, 95, 105, 110, 111, 112, 114, 158

R

Rahner, Karl 49, 52, 57

Rahner's Rule 57

reason 58, 60, 68, 70, 74, 95, 102, 103, 104, 105, 106, 108, 114, 120, 144, 158

Redeemer 65, 66, 139, 158

Reformers 51

relationality 77, 86, 93, 147

responsibility 30, 58, 66, 74, 107, 142, 144, 149, 155, 158

restoration 28

resurrection 14, 22, 41, 43, 62, 66, 116, 133, 156, 157

revelation 17, 32, 39, 41, 56, 57,
58, 60, 61, 63, 68, 78, 79,
100, 124, 127
    biblical 96, 114
    full 60, 85, 97, 110, 136, 138
    general 58, 59, 60, 127
    God's self-revelation 60, 64,
    74, 78, 89, 138, 154
    holistic 38
    New Testament 38, 64
    preincarnate 35
    progressive 55, 57
    special 59, 60, 127
    Trinitarian 64
Richard of St. Victor 52, 76, 83
righteousness 74, 92, 93, 95, 105,
110, 112, 113, 114, 117, 158
role 27, 66, 75, 115, 118, 135, 136,
137, 139, 154, 158, 159
    baptism 23
    Bridegroom 65
    Creator 65, 123, 132, 138,
    139, 140, 143, 148, 157
    Economic Trinity 137
    Father 16, 28, 29, 69, 71,
    132, 140, 148, 151.
    See Father
    Friend 65, 158
    Husband 65, 90, 136
    Judge. See Judge
    King 115, 147, 148, 149, 151.
    See also King
    metaphorical 125, 135, 139,
    147
    metaphysical 139, 147
    of personal freedom 118
    of reason 103
    Personal Revealer. See Per-
    sonal Revealer
    Physician 65
    Priest. See Priest
    Prophet 65, 138
    Redeemer. See Redeemer
    Shepherd. See Shepherd
    Son 14, 45, 157
    Spirit 16, 17, 19, 52, 59

Teacher 65, 138, 158, 167
Warrior 65
rûah 29
van Ruysbroeck, Jan 52

S

Sabellius of Ptolemais 43
sanctification
    full 63, 152
    progressive 63
Shema 124
Shepherd 65, 136, 138, 139, 158
Son of God 13, 14, 34, 36, 41, 42,
45, 47, 88, 100, 116, 117, 131,
138, 143, 152
Son of Man 138
Stauffer, Ethelbert 91
subordinationism 45, 46, 73
Summa Theologica 85, 134
supranatural 16, 80, 91, 118, 126,
131, 134, 142, 155

T

Teacher. See role: Teacher
theandric union 138
theism 115, 117, 121, 122, 128, 132
    open 121, 131, 132
The Language and Imagery of the
Bible 136
theodicy 142
Theodotus 42, 43
theophanies 38
Thomas Aquinas 85
Torrance, T. F. 11, 22, 46, 47, 49,
52, 54, 56, 57, 59, 60, 68, 73,
74, 75, 76, 79, 97, 100, 101,
107, 146, 150

transcendence 44, 102, 103, 104, 118, 123, 125, 128, 132, 133, 141, 151

triadic form 22

Trinitarian theism 121, 122, 128

Trinity
consubstantial 54
Economic 55, 56, 57, 58, 60, 61, 64, 65, 66, 67, 68, 69, 76, 77, 78, 91, 92, 97, 110, 114, 134, 135, 137, 139, 140, 147, 152, 153
immanent 57
Ontological 50, 55, 56, 57, 68, 69, 70, 77, 79, 92, 93, 97, 105, 106, 114, 132, 139, 140, 146
relational 105
social 98

triunity 36, 37, 73, 124

truth 20, 33, 47, 49, 59, 61, 74, 92, 93, 95, 105, 106, 110, 111, 112, 114, 120, 122, 137, 138, 158

U

unity 27, 31, 32, 42, 49, 50, 51, 53, 57, 64, 65, 66, 67, 72, 73, 74, 75, 76, 80, 88, 96, 99, 100, 107, 124

V

Virgin Mary 16
Vriezen, Theodore 88

W

Wainwright, Geoffrey 19, 101

Wesley, John 52, 144, 157, 162, 163

will 12, 16, 17, 18, 20, 24, 26, 27, 28, 31, 36, 37, 41, 48, 58, 66, 70, 74, 76, 82, 85, 87, 88, 89, 90, 95, 96, 98, 100, 102, 104, 105, 106, 108, 110, 111, 112, 113, 116, 117, 119, 121, 123, 128, 129, 136, 137, 139, 143, 144, 145, 151, 153, 154, 157, 158, 159, 163

William of St. Thierry 52

wisdom 28, 32, 33, 38, 45, 74, 95, 116, 117, 118, 122, 123, 144, 157, 159, 162

Wood, Skevington 31, 88, 90, 111

Word of God 31, 32, 33, 43, 65, 111

worship 20, 22, 23, 28, 35

Wright, N. T. 14, 155

Y

Yahweh 10, 13, 15, 31, 32, 33, 34, 35, 36, 37, 56, 64, 65, 110, 137

Z

Zizioulas, John D. 52, 73, 98, 99, 107

Made in the USA
Columbia, SC
23 June 2025

59786025R00100